Praise for
The Wind That Destroys

"All of us who have suffered deep loss will find here profound affirmation, beautifully expressed, strongly thought, and honestly lived that the wind does blow—sometimes cold and cruel—but then again deep and healing. Here is true theology lived, practiced, and passed on. Read it and the wind may blow freshly for you, too."

> —LEIGHTON FORD, president of Leighton Ford Ministries, Charlotte, North Carolina

"A true companion for the saga of grief. Stephen Broyles does not explain or fix—he seriously shares."

> —JOHN R. CLAYPOOL, Episcopal priest and author of *Trades of a Fellow Struggler*

"We affirm Stephen Broyles's deep lessons—having experienced them in our son's death by murder. We understand, yet we do not understand, for each grief takes us down a singular path. Broyles's journey and insights gently guide in that deepest experience of all life."

> —JERRY E. WHITE, Ph.D., president of The Navigators, and MARY A. WHITE, author of *Harsh Grief, Gentle Hope*

"Stephen Broyles, though a theologian, speaks to you simply as a father, husband, and man whose faith was supremely tested. There is healing inside for the writer *and* the reader."

> —DALE R. WARD, executive producer, World Christian Broadcasting

"This book is a poignantly powerful picture of human existence—joy and sadness, life and death, faith and fear, pleasure and pain, acceptance and rejection, and suffering and redemption. It is affirming to be reminded that God is with us."

—THE REVEREND DR. CHRISTOPHER M. HAMLIN, pastor
and author of *Behind the Stained Glass: A History of Sixteenth Street Baptist Church*

"These reflections on the presence and absence of God amid suffering, pain, and death draw on lessons learned from Scripture, theology, and spirituality. Stephen Broyles reminds us of our common mortality even as he calls us to cling to hope."

—BILL J. LEONARD, dean of Wake Forest University
Divinity School

the Wind THAT DESTROYS and HEALS

Trusting the God *of* Sorrow and Joy

STEPHEN E. BROYLES

SHAW BOOKS
an imprint of WATERBROOK PRESS

The Wind That Destroys and Heals
A SHAW BOOK
PUBLISHED BY WATERBROOK PRESS
2375 Telstar Drive, Suite 160
Colorado Springs, Colorado 80920
A division of Random House, Inc.

ISBN 1-57856-653-3

Library of Congress Cataloging-in-Publication Data
Broyles, Stephen E.
    The wind that destroys and heals : trusting the God of sorrow and joy / Stephen E. Broyles.—1st ed.
    p. cm.
    Includes bibliographical references.
    ISBN 1-57856-653-3
    1. Consolation. I. Title.
BV4905.3 B76 2003
248.8'6—dc21

2002152723

Printed in the United States of America
2003—First Edition

10 9 8 7 6 5 4 3 2 1

Τῇ ἐπιτερπῶν ὡρῶν μνήμη

Contents

Acknowledgments

During the time when this book was passing through various stages on the way to its present form, I benefited from good editorial guidance and encouragement. I wish to express my deep appreciation to Ramona Cramer Tucker, Mary Horner Collins, Vinita Hampton Wright, Annette LaPlaca, Dan Penwell, Bruce Barbour of Literary Management Group, and Ron Lee of WaterBrook Press for their receptiveness, optimism, and sound advice. I express my gratitude to two local churches, Magnolia and Cahaba Valley, and one distant one, the Basler Gemeinde, for their influence on my life during a difficult time. They perhaps did not know how much I needed them nor how good they were for me. I am grateful to Beverly Dowdy, first that she was Elizabeth's friend, then that she and Ken were mine. Finally, I give thanks for my wife, Sharon, who arrived after a long time, but at the right time.

I sometimes hold it half a sin
    To put in words the grief I feel;
    For words, like Nature, half reveal
And half conceal the Soul within.

But, for the unquiet heart and brain,
    A use in measured language lies;
    The sad mechanic exercise,
Like dull narcotics, numbing pain.

In words, like weeds, I'll wrap me o'er,
    Like coarsest clothes against the cold;
    But that large grief which these enfold
Is given in outline and no more.

—ALFRED, LORD TENNYSON

MY END IN MY BEGINNING

The book which the reader now holds in his hands, from one end to
the other, as a whole and in its details…treats of the advance from evil
to good…from darkness to daylight…from Hell to Heaven.

—VICTOR HUGO, *Les Misérables*

In the book of Job, the wind both destroys and heals. The wind destroys
Job's children, and this terrible loss plunges Job into deepest suffering. And
yet the wind is also the place where Job hears a healing word from God.

In the Bible, the wind is a symbol of the impermanence of human life
and the enlivening power of God. A psalm tells us that God is compassionate toward humankind, for "he remembered that they were but flesh,
a passing breeze that does not return."[1] And yet God can enliven even the
lifeless. In Ezekiel's vision, the wind sweeps over the valley of dry bones,
and they are brought to life by the breath and Spirit of God.[2] Again, the
wind is the force that brings life to an end: "The wind blows over it and
it is gone, and its place remembers it no more."[3] And yet the wind is the
birthing place of the Spirit: "The wind blows wherever it pleases. You hear
its sound, but you cannot tell where it comes from or where it is going.
So it is with everyone born of the Spirit."[4]

We must all face the wind. It is dark, alien, and irresistibly powerful. In it are death and extinction. Yet it is possible to face the wind and to find in the experience profound religious value—to be, indeed, reborn.

One cold February my family became engulfed in the wind and darkness of my wife's illness. It took her life on Christmas Day four years later. Our two young children and I survived and continue to recover.

The years in the wind changed me. I began to see new significance in biblical spirituality and to know its value when it comes to us amid our unbearable hurts. I have become alive in a new way to familiar images: the laments of the psalmists and their decision to use whatever life there was for praise; Job, both destroyed and healed by the wind, trusting God even when God seemed untrustworthy; Jesus in Gethsemane praying to the God who had seemingly forsaken him and yet finding through faith in this same God the validation of life and faith.

During our family's dark time and afterward, I kept a journal. In hundreds of pages of cramped and erratic handwriting, I uttered my barbaric yawp against the illness and its effect on our lives, and I confronted the perplexities of mortality and faith.

This book is not a transcription of that journal. They are two separate and different things. The book has come from my present state of mind, while the journal has supplied memory and rough-hewn lumber—ideas that are here planed smooth. So you must not think that in these pages I will afflict you with grief-work that is properly my own. Rather, I will try to say something about the very real possibility of trust in a world that sometimes gives us little reason to trust.

There is a good deal of narrative in these pages, for I want you to know that this book is not mere speculation. Life is being dealt with. Ideas that we work out intellectually without reference to brute fact often prove feeble and empty when put against the hard shape and shove of reality. Some of my finest ideas have vanished in this way without a trace. It is the experience we call "being left speechless." By including narrative in this book, I intend to recall us to our true business: living a considered life.

In response to the narrative, I have done my philosophizing. Or perhaps I should call it theologizing, for after all, I am a Christian theologian by trade. But I will not urge my viewpoint upon you. I will not tell you that you must think as I do. I will simply tell what it has been like for me, and I will share what I have been able to put together out of all this. After all, to be a Christian is not to be safe or certain or unassailable or any of those other things people of faith often try to be, but to be as bewildered and slammed about as anyone else—and also to discover the redemptive pattern encoded in the experience of suffering.

I offer no quick-fix theology or easy answers. In fact, I offer no help at all in avoiding or lessening life's pain. To propose to take another's grief so easily away is to trivialize it, to make it a small thing. But it is not small. It is crushing and monstrous. What I offer is a voice crying in the night, the sense of human community in suffering, and the knowledge that healing and wholeness can be born of pain and sorrow.

THE DESCENT
OF NIGHT

I fancied I had some constancy of mind because I could bear my own sufferings, but found through the sufferings of others I could be weakened like a child.

—SARAH FIELDING, *The Adventures of David Simple*

While we were living them, the nights and days seemed endless. Now they seem as one night into which memory has poured all the darkness and bewilderment of those nights and days.

"Do you want me to bring you coffee?"

"No," I said. "Not now."

The nurse closed the wide, heavy door behind her as she left. The sound of its closing was deep and portentous, a sound like the earth opening up.

I pulled my chair closer to the bed and sat in the quiet semidarkness. Elizabeth slept under a white cotton blanket, breathing through slack mouth. Oxygen bubbled from an outlet on the wall and hissed through plastic tubing. Outside a light rain was falling. Its steady hush made the silence of the room grow deeper.

A rumbling came from the hall, and I turned, expecting technicians to wheel some ponderous piece of equipment into the room. But the door remained closed. This time the rumbling passed us by.

I turned again in my chair. Elizabeth breathed quietly in her sleep, and her chapped lower lip hung loosely to one side. I sat still and tried to sort it out, but it would not sort. I was another Jacob, wrestling another angel who would not go down. I was glad that Elizabeth was asleep: On this night it was too frightening to be awake.

It was Christmas Eve. We had hoped, two weeks before, that Elizabeth would be home again by now. As the days passed, hope began to fade until it finally vanished altogether.

"I don't expect to go home," she said. "Too many things are wrong with me, and there is no way to fix them all."

I called and arranged for my parents to bring Stephanie and John to the hospital. We met in the waiting room, and I brought the children in separately. The visits were short and quiet. Then I brought them in together to say good-bye. The last words they heard from their mother were words of love.

Stephanie was ten and she had questions. In the waiting room she asked me, "Why is it so hard for Mother to breathe?"

"Her lungs are filling up."

"Why don't they stop it?"

"They are trying."

"They can take some x-rays to see what's wrong, and then they can stop it."

"That's what they are doing, but it's not that easy."

"Will they be able to stop it?"

"They will try very hard."

John was four years younger. He asked, "Is Mother coming home in two or three more days?" His voice was even and direct.

"I don't think so, John."

"I'm tired of being at other people's houses," he said. "It's been two weeks. I see you twenty minutes at night and twenty minutes in the morning, and little kids that don't see their parents forget what they look like."

He was not angry. He was not pouting. He was simply stating facts. When he had stated them, he looked steadfastly at a fixed point in space. He would look at that point until he got an answer. This I knew from six years' unvarying experience.

"I've missed you, John."

"I've missed you, too."

Elizabeth thought much about the children. She told me she wanted to be there as they grew up. She wanted to see them through childhood and see them graduate and marry and raise their own children. She wanted nothing extraordinary. Only that.

We whispered together in the dark. "This," she said, "is our final time together. We need to get our lives worked out."

I asked, "Do you forgive me for all the bad things I've done?"

She nodded. "And do you me?"

"Yes."

She was quiet. She breathed shallow, feeble breaths, and I listened for every one. After a time, she said, "If I don't make it, I want you to know one thing. You have done everything you could do."

"So have you."

"Thank you."

Sitting in the darkness, listening to her breathing and her occasional words, I did not feel noble or exemplary. I felt a coward. I was terrified to be there, and I was terrified not to be. I wanted to be in two places at once. I wanted to be with the children, talking with Stephanie about her questions and holding John when he was afraid. And I wanted to be with Elizabeth, too, sitting in my chair by her bed. That had been my place through everything she had endured, and it was my place now. I was the one who knew what she wanted, who could admit with her what was happening, and against whom she could vent her rage. How could I not be there? And yet how could I be?

A past of pain and gritted teeth and relentless terrors crowded my memory, and a future of desolation and fear and bewilderment crowded my imagination. The only hurt that can be endured is the present hurt. And yet memory and imagination could not be held back. Together with the horror of the present moment, they produced a hurt beyond enduring, an adversary who would not go down. I told myself that if it was possible to bear this, it was only by bearing each present moment as it came. A severe dilemma. It is the only possible way, and it, too, is impossible.

Later in the night they brought a cot and placed it near Elizabeth's bed. I lay down in my clothes and shoes and listened to the sound of her breathing. Whether we would both be there in the morning was more than anyone could know.

The cot was close to the bed, touching it. Eventually I slept and dreamed that I was lying on a cot in my shoes and clothes. I was close to her bed, listening to the sound of her breathing. In my dream I knew that someone or something was outside the door, wanting to come in, ready to force its way. I heard a menacing sound, like thunder: a heavy, ponderous sound, a sound like the earth opening up. The door, solid and heavy, was swinging open, and I felt the icy blast of a driving wind. In my dream I cried, "Death is at the door! Death is at the door!" My hair stood on end all over my head and down my neck. I woke up trembling.

The room was quiet except for the soft bubbling of the oxygen and the faint sound of Elizabeth's breathing. Then I was dreaming again. Thunder. The icy blast. The cry: "Death is at the door!" Terror. Trembling. And I listened again to the sound of her breathing.

I prayed in the darkness and two people spoke. One was the man I was at that moment, chilled by the darkness and terror, reasoning against reason in a vain attempt to understand. The other was the child who was still somehow in me, longing for sunlight and pleasant grass and the safe feeling of a big hand reaching down to a small hand, for the child felt the man's terror and helplessness and utter bewilderment.

"Dear God," I prayed—that is, the man and the child prayed together —"Dear Jesus. She is in such trauma and anguish! Dear God, have mercy. Sweet Jesus, have mercy. Dear God, have mercy. Give her peace and rest. Let the anguish and agony and violence give way to peace and calm. Dear God dear God dear God dear God dear God. Grant this one mercy, that if it must come—and how can it not come?—may it be a passage through tranquillity and peace."

Chapter 1

THE MEETING OF PAST AND FUTURE

Making Sense of Our Story

I have been torn between the times, the order of which I do not know, and my thoughts, even the inmost and deepest places of my soul, are mangled by various commotions until I shall flow together into thee, purged and molten in the fire of thy love.

—AUGUSTINE OF HIPPO, *Confessions*

John ran out the back door wearing the football uniform Santa had brought him. I picked him up and walked with him to the house.

Stephanie was just inside the door. She knew. We had all come back from the hospital, and she knew we would not all come back until there was no longer reason to stay.

I carried my son into the house and asked Stephanie to come with us. She would not. She knew, but she would not let me say the words to her.

John and I sat down, and I told him the story.

"In the middle of the night, your mother became a lot worse. She couldn't breathe. I sat by her and laid my head on the pillow by hers and listened to her breathing. It got weaker and weaker and fainter and fainter."

"She's dying," John said softly.

"Her breathing became so weak that I could barely hear it, and then I couldn't hear it any more at all. Then a nurse came in, and then a doctor came in."

"She's dead."

"Yes."

John lay down and cried. After a time he sat up, quiet and speaking softly again.

"I guess everything is useless now, isn't it, Dad?"

"That's the way it feels."

For the rest of the day, Stephanie would not hear it from me. There were too many people, and there was too much to do. At bedtime, when everyone had left and John was asleep, she and I talked, although not directly about what had happened.

Next day, in the evening, the house was quiet again except for us three. Stephanie let it be known that she wanted to hear the story now. By the time I finished, it was clear that already, while they had played with their Christmas toys, John had told her, word for word, the story as I had told it to him.

THE STORY OF JACOB'S NAME

During the months following Elizabeth's death, I often thought of the story of Jacob's wrestling with the man all night. The story had points of contact with our own story.

Jacob had reached a point of turning, and he knew it. For twenty years he had lived in the old country, the land of his ancestors, where he had fled for his life from his brother, Esau. In the old country, he struck a somewhat adversarial arrangement with his Uncle Laban, acquired wives and wealth, and eventually rivaled Laban's position in the family. Finally, Jacob had to flee the old country, pursued by his uncle, and set out for the new country, where his brother waited, plotting who knows what kind of revenge. Well into the journey, at the downslope of the Jabbok River, Jacob divided his caravan into two groups and sent them on ahead, while he remained alone. In the night, a man wrestled with him until the breaking of the day. Neither emerged as the clear winner, but at dawn Jacob had the new name, Israel, and he walked away limping.

The center and meaning of the story is symbolized by the renaming of the patriarch. At birth he had been called Jacob, literally *Heel-Grabber,* a Hebrew idiom meaning "deceiver." Now he is called Israel, *God-Striver,* because he has striven with God and with men and has prevailed.[1] Crisis has divided his life into two parts, and each part has its own name.

We live out, in our own lives, a story similar to Jacob's. Our lives are broken by crisis. We feel the sting of adversity's dark wind in our face and find ourselves falling headlong into the abyss. We wrestle with the angel all through the night and limp away at the coming of the dawn. We find in Jacob's story a pattern for our task of finding a new name for ourselves, a name that will give some measure of meaning both to the horrors that pursue us from the past and to the new understanding that we take with us into the future.

For it was not the same Jacob who walked on. The years in the old country had changed him, and at the Jabbok he realized it. Twenty years before, he had passed this way, and God had spoken to him in the night. Next morning he raised a stone on end and made the following prayer: "If God will be with me and will watch over me on this journey I am taking and will give me food to eat and clothes to wear so that I return safely to my father's house, then the LORD will be my God and this stone that I have set up as a pillar will be God's house, and of all that you give me I will give you a tenth."[2] Really now, we must admit that this is not much of a prayer. "Dear Lord, put food in my mouth and clothes on my back and keep me from getting my fool throat slit, and you can be my God and have this rock for a house." Well; at least it is a prayer. Often my prayers are not much better.

Now, after the experiences of twenty years, Jacob is on the road again and has once more reached a crisis point that means life and death. He has begun to see things differently. "O God," he prays, "I am unworthy of all the kindness and faithfulness you have shown your servant. I had only my staff when I crossed this Jordan, but now I have become two groups."[3] He goes on to plead for deliverance, and he calls to mind God's promise. But it is clear that something has happened in Heel-Grabber's heart. In the night of his trouble and distress, he confesses that God is kind and faithful. He knew this before, perhaps; now he realizes it and places himself—not without struggle!—in the hands of this God.

THE STORY OF US ALL

It is a universal story. We descend through confusion and bewilderment and suffering, wondering whether there is any end to it. We arrive finally at a turning point, often so severe it threatens to undo us. Then—whether through our own will or not, I cannot explain, but certainly not through our own power—we find ourselves being lifted upward and outward to something larger and wiser.

Life is a complicated, overlapping pattern of these downs and ups: the downward movement to pain, sorrow, suffering, and ultimately, death; the upward movement to relief, blessedness, joy, deliverance, and life. The downward movement is true of both the life of faith and the life without faith. Never mind that some believers in God reject misfortune and suffering as unthinkable in a life of genuine faith. They are simply wrong. This world is not, after all, heaven yet, and the sooner we realize that, the better we will get on. But what we must realize, too, is that God is just as present and just as trustworthy in the downward movement as in the upward.

The story of Jacob helped me understand this, as well as the stories of the psalmists, of Job, and most of all, the story of Jesus, which is the Very Story. The stories that inform my life come from the Bible. They connect my story to the Ultimate Story. If they are subplots to the ultimate narrative, my life is a subplot to them, and in this way, my life participates in ultimate meaning. Stories from history or literature might also serve this purpose—but only so far as they are reflections of the Very Story.

The universal story is, in a way, our essential self. I not only *have* a story, I *am* a story. When I look at old family photographs, I see myself as a toddler standing in the sun beside Grandmother's lawn chair. I see a two-year-old in cap and sweater. I see a boy selling violets from an upturned fruit basket, then a young man on a ladder picking apples, then a grown man sprawled in an Adirondack chair. The photographs show growth and change. They tell a story.

No matter what our background, and no matter what our advantages, our story eventually will bring us to times when life is painful. When we were children becoming young men and women, we discovered that our parents were flawed and imperfect, that the world was not always safe and welcoming, that our innocent view of reality had to change. It was a painful time. If we are parents of children on the verge of young adulthood, we discover that we must let them go, and it is painful to give up our children to a world full of harm. In midlife we discover that the range of our potential, once seemingly limitless, has narrowed to a meager handful of options. Henry David Thoreau put it this way: "The youth gets together his materials to build a bridge to the moon, or perchance a palace or temple on the earth, and at length the middle-aged man concludes to build a wood-shed with them."[4] As if settling for the woodshed were not enough, we must sooner or later accept that youthful beauty and vigor are waning, that powers we once had are lessening, that life does not last forever. We must face the deaths of people we love, people whose lives were inexpressibly valuable to us. At last, we must face our own death and the apparent loss of everything for which we have striven.

The pain of growth can seem at times more than we can bear. And yet, because life is story, we are more than our pain. At any present moment, our essential self is made up not only of what we are now but of everything we have ever been. And to carry it a step further, our essential self as God sees us must also include everything we will ever be.

Our lives become meaningful when we view them as complete shapes, including both life's downward and upward movements. To see only the downward trend to annihilation and ruin is to despair needlessly. To think only of serenity and peace is to ignore a significant portion of human experience. We will never get it right as long as we select only a part of ourselves and view that part as if it were the whole. We must embrace it all. Because of where we are in the process, that means embracing a past whose memory often brings us pain, while yet summoning the courage to step into the dark wind of the unhappened future.

Exactly here we face one of life's dilemmas. Life presents us with two kinds of experiences. One kind upholds human aspirations and sustains our belief that the best things we strive for are noble, beautiful, and good. The other dashes our hopes and leaves us weak and powerless. It confronts us with the fact that from one moment to the next fortunes can reverse, and we are helpless to do much about it. Events that at first seem random, mindless, and purposeless develop into a systematic assault on everything we hold valuable. A bone marrow test shows tumor. The course of events becomes unpredictable yet inexorable. Life skids on the verge of insanity, and we look down into the sickening depths of a void that swallows up values, both human and divine, and yet remains always a void.

I know of no way adequately to account for the presence of this void in the universe. The Bible assumes the existence of evil, as it assumes God's existence, without argument or explanation. I know only that the waves of the void lap persistently on the shores of human experience, and we encounter it in everything that is random, purposeless, and absurd. The void is the realm of chaos from which meaning and value are forever banished.

The more we assert human dignity and worth, the more we are disturbed by the presence of the void. When we assert, too, the goodness and power of God, the power of evil presents to faith a persistent and irresistible trial. The story that gives meaning and purpose to our lives does not merely tell of happy ascent into bliss and enlightenment. It tells also of descent into suffering, terror, and desolation. It is perhaps easy enough for us to accept the happy ascent. But what are we to do with the part of our story that takes us down into pain and sorrow? How do we deal with terror and bewilderment? How do we bear the words and sights that will not leave our memory until, by some kind of exorcism, they are driven out?

Somehow we must find a way to accept human suffering and mortality without losing our faith in all that is beautiful and strong and good. Or to put it another way, to trust God even when he seems untrustworthy.

THE LIMITS OF TIME

The way of our lives is a journey through time, but time itself has little power to heal. Because we accumulate experiences and carry them inside us, no amount of time working alone will make them distant or lessen their pain.

Ordinarily, we think of events in time as advancing steadily upon us from the future, crossing the razor-sharp boundary line of the present, and receding from us into the past. We especially tend to think that when an event has crossed over into the past, it continues to recede forever, becoming more and more distant. But it is not so. That may be true of chronological distance, but it is not necessarily true of psychological distance. Time measured by the clock is not the same as time measured by the heart.

Friends once told me of an English woman and an American serviceman who fell in love during the Second World War and planned to marry. But the man was killed in an accident shortly after the war ended, and by the time the woman learned of it, his body had been buried in the United States. Thirty years passed. The woman kept in touch with the man's family during those years, and finally she came to America to visit them. She asked to be taken to the man's grave, and there she wept as if those thirty years had not elapsed since she had last seen him.

Despite the passage of time, our past experiences remain immediate, either because we remember them or because, like moist clay, we bear the imprint of having lived through them. Time does not heal us. After the downward plunge into the abyss, healing does not begin until we ascend the uphill slope through the hard work of remembering and forgiving.

FORGIVING THE PAST

It was my job in the slow months following Elizabeth's death to remember the terror and pain and grief and odium and rage and weakness and the last feeble gesture and the heaviness and coldness. I had to remember them again and again until I could remember and remain myself while remembering. When I could do that, I found that two important things became possible: I could think of the past without being hurt by it, and I could forgive the past for being what it was. *Forgive,* because to release the hurts of the past is an act very like forgiveness.

Forgiveness is never easy. We have all done things the badness of which we now feel and for which we must both be forgiven and forgive ourselves.

The list of my own atrocities is long, and it contains who knows how many acts I could dislike myself for. Even if I did not fully know an act's badness at the time, I know it now. A discord sets up between the me of the present and the me of the past, resulting in blame, disparagement, and sometimes loathing. I have had to learn both to accept forgiveness and to forgive myself. When I am able to do that, peace returns. I do not dislike the person I am now because a person I once was chose badness instead of goodness. I forgive him, indeed *must* forgive him, in order to be whole.

Forgiving the people we were in the past for what they have done prepares us for something yet harder. We must forgive the people we are for having had the unspeakable experiences whose recollection causes pain. We must forgive ourselves not only for having been wicked and cowardly and proud but also for having been powerless to resist adversity and terror and desolation. It is not easy to forgive the past. It is not easy to forgive misfortune. But if ever the future is to hold anything good and noble and beautiful, it must be a future cleansed by forgiveness of the past.

FACING THE FUTURE

The night when Elizabeth lay dying was our darkest moment of anguish and despair. The past contained nothing but terrors, and the terrors pursued us relentlessly. Future terrors lay ahead—death, desolation, and emptiness. We knew it and we were right. We trembled while the wind blew hard against the door, and we were powerless when it forced its way in.

But that moment in the darkness did not last forever. There came a time when it was over, and the past included *everything* again, not just the terrors. The future, too, took on a different look. It still seemed empty, because it had not yet happened. But it held out once more the possibility of goodness.

Possibility, mind you. Not certainty. The awareness remained that we are forever poised on the edge, facing the wind of the unhappened future, not knowing what it will bring.

This is what it was like. I grew up where it seldom snowed, but I wanted it to snow again and again. We children believed that if we wanted too much for the snow to fall, it would not. If we watched it snowing, it would stop. So we played by the window, hoping for the snow, wanting with all our hearts to see the first flake, and yet we hardly dared to look lest our wanting it would make it go away.

That is the way facing the future seemed to me as I emerged from the terror of the darkness. I began again to hope, but I could not so soon forget that the future can exercise its own irresistible autonomy.

At different moments the future seemed to be everything anyone has ever said about it—both the welcome and the dreaded. That night when the future crouched at the door, it seemed as hard and unequivocal as the present, as inevitable as any determinist would care to make it. At other moments it seemed to include the infinite realm of labyrinthine futures from a Jorge Luis Borges story: "an infinite series of times, in a growing, dizzying net of divergent, convergent and parallel times."[5] At other moments the future seemed to have no existence at all and yet to be known to God as perfectly as our own thoughts are known to us (a concept Augustine accepted but by which he was nonetheless puzzled). Or the future seemed like Charles Dickens's third spirit: dark, hooded, and silent, his hand pointing onward along the path. At still other moments it seemed to be Jean-Paul Sartre's future of possibilities with which imagination endows the present and from which we must choose a single one.

There must be numerous futures, and the one that happens is shaped by many things: the physical nature of the universe for one, and the exercise of free will on the part of sentient beings for another. And yet, when it will have happened, it will be but one future after all. Because time is a continuous process, the future will be an unfolding from the present, just as the present is from the past. The wind blowing to us from the future does not come from some foreign and discontinuous order of reality; it comes from a future to which we will in some ways have contributed, but before which we will in other ways have remained helpless.

We cannot know which of the possible futures will happen, but we can know that we will enter the future taking ourselves with us. We will not meet the icy wind utterly naked, for we will have the degree of preparedness that our past has given us. We will not meet it utterly powerless, for even in its worst moments, we will at least choose our inner response. And we will not meet it alone, for in the very act of wrestling the angel who will not go down, we will encounter the God who changes our name.

Take courage. The wall against which you are driven will become a door opening outward. The depth of your misery will become your point of turning.

Chapter 2

AT THE POINT
OF TURNING

Finding Light in the Darkness

That all the clay of you, all of the dross of you,
May yield to the fire of you,
Till the fire is nothing but light!…
Nothing but light!

—EDGAR LEE MASTERS

I pulled the chain on the lamp, and the top of my desk was flooded with light. It was three in the morning. I picked up my pen, entered the date in my journal, and began to write:

Three months. I have finally cleaned out the closet. I put away the
Christmas ornaments long ago, a box of Kleenex under my arm,
alternately wrapping ornaments and blowing my nose. I cleaned
out the kitchen cabinet next. It was full of alcohol preps and swabs
and op-site bandages and sterile gauze and Huber needles and
small white pills in teacups. Last of all, I have done the closet. I

found a bag at the very back. It was a shopping bag from Lucerne, dangling from a coat hanger. The sight of it brought back the memory of beautiful days. I wondered what Elizabeth might have put in this bag and hung far back behind the clothes. I opened it and looked inside, and I crumpled into a heap on the floor. I lay on my side and pulled my knees to my chest and remained there for a long time. I had found her hair.

SIFTING THE PAST

In the months following Elizabeth's death, my children and I faced the task of sorting through the past and deciding what to take with us into the future. It was a difficult time, this sorting: what to keep and what to let go of, what to carry with us as we crossed the Jabbok and what to leave behind.

Stephanie and John may one day write their own stories of what it was like for them to find their way. I can tell no one's story but my own. The tasks confronting me were these: to endure the memory of four years during which a fellow human suffered pain, helplessness, and terror; to face the mortality of a person only half finished with life, who wanted to go on to raise her children, to work at her job, to touch and gaze upon the things she loved, and yet, despite all efforts, could not live to do those things; to survive the violent, almost demonic destruction of health, well-being, career, marriage, parenthood, and life itself. What to take with me from this terrible past, and what to leave behind!

So important was it to part with the past while taking its good things along with us, that the children and I acted it out in a little ceremony. One morning at breakfast I said, "Today would have been your mother's birthday. We will have a special supper, and then we will turn balloons loose in the backyard." That night we sat down to chicken chow mein, with the explanation that their mother used to like it, and peach pie, which needed no explanation.

During supper I said, "I'll tell something, and then each of you tell something. When your mother and I were first married, we lived in a small apartment near the high school. When they played football on Friday nights, we could hear the band, and we could hear the loudspeaker announcing the plays, so we never had to buy tickets. To furnish our apartment, we borrowed a refrigerator, and we bought a secondhand stove for fifteen dollars, and I brought my chair and piano from home. That is how we started housekeeping."

Stephanie said, "I remember that every morning she would come in and wake me up, singing, 'Dummy line, rise and shine on the dummy line.'"

John said, "I remember that she would give me gummy bears when I could say my colors in German."

We took the balloons outside and wrote words on them—private words unknown to the others—and released them from the driveway. It was an overcast day and getting on toward dark. The balloons vanished quickly.

It was not a sentimental ceremony. After all, it was lived in the present moment, and these were real children, not actors in a film, and they had been taken away from homework and jam boxes and video games, and they were eager to get back to them. Neither cared for chicken chow mein, and releasing the balloons became a race to see whose would go up the fastest. And yet they understood the evening well enough. It was both a remembering and a letting go.

THINGS OF THE SPIRIT

It was clear that the most important things to take with us into the future were not material objects but things of the spirit. These alone are truly valuable, for we can add them to the patterned mosaic of bewilderment and understanding that in an imperfect world passes for wisdom. Engulfed by the wind and having been both annihilated and reborn by its power, I discovered a growing readiness to embrace the things of the spirit in a way that was new to me.

I remember the day I cleaned out the dresser drawers.

In the drawer by the bed I found Elizabeth's Bible. I opened it and noticed that she had underlined passages in the Psalms. The first words to strike my eye were these: "Listen to my cry, for I am in desperate need."[1] The words expressed her thought exactly, during those nights and days of suffering and uncertainty, although the words had come to her across a huge distance of time and space.

Then there was this plea: "Do not withhold your mercy from me, O LORD.... For troubles without number surround me."[2] Yes. That is the way it was, especially toward the last, when everything inside her was going wrong, and it appeared that even God's mercies had reached their end.

Then this confident hope: "The LORD will sustain him on his sickbed and restore him from his bed of illness."[3] No. That had not happened. And yet, in spite of that, there was this surprising affirmation: "I praise you...your works are wonderful, I know that full well."[4]

Finally I found these astonishing verses:

I am bowed down and brought very low;
    all day long I go about mourning.
My back is filled with searing pain;
    there is no health in my body.
I am feeble and utterly crushed;
    I groan in anguish of heart.[5]

The words described precisely how Elizabeth had felt during the final months of her illness.

The underlining in the Psalms evidently meant that Elizabeth had borrowed language from these ancient Hebrew poems to express her own feelings of sorrow and helplessness and her feeling for God. I read through other psalms and noticed—as if for the first time—how many allusions there were to suffering and illness and death. The book of Psalms contains not only the merry shouts of Israelites clapping their hands and making a joyful noise before the Lord. It contains also the groans and pleas of the sick and the frightened and the dying. I had known that before. Now, I realized it for the first time.

What was it in these psalms that drew Elizabeth to mark them and turn to them again and again? What was common to the experience of an ancient Hebrew poet lying ill on his pallet and a woman of modern times lying ill on her bed? I wanted to know, so I read the Psalms as never before.

The Psalms led me on to the book of Job. When you are ready to listen to what the Bible says about illness and suffering, you come very quickly to Job. I found more of Elizabeth's underlining here. As in the Psalms, some of the marked verses were intensely personal: "Why is light given to those in misery,…to those who long for death that does not come?"[6] "When I lie down I think, 'How long before I get up?' The night drags on, and I toss till dawn."[7] "I despise my life.… Let me alone; my days have no meaning."[8] And alongside such cries from the depths of misery was this: "The LORD gave and the LORD has taken away; may the name of the LORD be praised."[9]

The underlining continued in the New Testament. Here, even more than in the Old Testament, suffering and praise are intertwined. And here for the first time, alongside both suffering and praise, is the name of Christ. "Praise be to the God and Father of our Lord Jesus Christ…who comforts us in all our troubles.… For just as the sufferings of Christ flow over into our lives, so also through Christ our comfort overflows."[10] "And the God of all grace, who called you to his eternal glory in Christ, after you have suffered a little while, will himself restore you and make you strong, firm and steadfast."[11]

THE POINT OF TURNING

For years I had been familiar with the Psalms, the story of Job and his encounter with God in the whirlwind, and the story of Jesus' agony in Gethsemane and the intense suffering that ended his life. Before, I had always read these stories with a certain detachment, a kind of objective interest. Now, I read them as a participant. I had known that these stories mattered a great deal for humankind. Now, I knew that they mattered a great deal for me.

Like Jacob, I had striven with God through the night and reached a point of turning. I found myself ready somehow, in a new way, to receive from the stories of the psalmists and Job and Jesus an empowering and an understanding that I did not possess before. A light had come on. A small light, but at three in the morning, one is grateful for any light at all.

At such points of turning, our understanding deepens and widens. Light reaches into corners of our selves that have long been hidden in shadow, and afterward, we are never again quite the same. Often the moment of turning follows catastrophe. I do not say that God sends catastrophes for this purpose. But catastrophes do come, and sometimes we do work our way through them to something meaningful, to something that propels us onward. I think I know how this happens. The catastrophe depletes our own inner resources and makes us ready to turn and look outward—it seems as if for the first time—and lay ourselves open to something vaster and wiser than ourselves. At the point of turning, we discover a resource we had not noticed earlier.

Although it sounds contradictory, catastrophe can reveal that hope and trust are upheld by the concrete reality of the working of God. If in the heart of darkness it seems otherwise to us—and it surely will—that is because, from our standpoint within time, the universal story of God is still in process of realization. And yet, the God who is beyond time has left the imprint of his story all about us, and we encounter it even when engulfed by the wind and darkness.

In the chapters that follow, we will look into the Psalms and the book of Job and the story of Jesus. I will tell what I can about the significance they have for life and faith when neither life nor faith seems possible. I cannot hope to give an easy, final answer to the question of suffering. No answer to any problem that matters is either easy or final, and the problem of suffering is the most obstinate problem of all. But there is a good in the universe alongside the bad, and it seeks to make itself known. I will try to set down the heart of what I have learned and show how it has helped me find my way.

Chapter 3

IN THE SHADOW
OF MORTALITY

Life and Death in the Psalms

> In black distress, I called my God,
> When I could scarce believe him mine.
> —HERMAN MELVILLE, *Moby Dick*

I will try to show what I have learned from the Psalms, those poems and prayers and hymns in which man addresses himself to God. My beginning place, however, is earlier in the Old Testament, in the book of Genesis, because this is where we find out who man is—this man who speaks to God in the Psalms.

THE CLAY MAN

In the second chapter of Genesis, there is the story of how God, working like a potter at his wheel, made a man out of clay and blew into him the breath of life. The story tells me what it means to be a clay man animated by the breath of God, and it tells me what it means to die.

First, I learn from this story that I am of the earth, that I am made of dust. Other things follow from this. I am physical. Part of what it means to be me is to have this body: this corn on my thumb (from playing the clarinet), this scar on my heel (from sticking it into some bicycle spokes), these arms and legs, this backside, this waist that is too high up to fit well into my trousers. I am frail. The clay man's most outrageous sin is the preposterous presumption that he is powerful. He struts to and fro on the earth, imagining that he is the Supreme Being. But no. To feel the frailty of dust is to be disinfected of presumption. I am temporary. I may live to age ninety-seven and stand on my head every day like father William. But one day my fire will go out, and people will look around for a brief, startled moment, and I will not be here anymore. This, too, is to be of the earth.

Second, I learn that not only am I of the earth, I am also of God. I am designed and crafted by him: "fearfully and wonderfully made," according to one of the psalms.[1] Because the clay man is of God, he possesses God's life, a property not inherent in dust, but put in by hand from the outside. Or more precisely, breathed out from the mouth of the Almighty. And the clay man embodies appetite, will, and desire, likewise not inherent in dust, but borrowed from God.

Third, I learn from this story something of what it means for the clay man to die. Popular sentiment often thinks of death as the soul's being set free from its prison house to float on benign vapors for all eternity. In contrast, the ancient Hebrew man pictures death as the life from God returning to God once more, and the clay-derived part of man returning to the dust once more. For Hebrew man, life without a body is not bliss; it is perdition, a kind of semiexistence in a land of shadows where one can no longer remember the Lord or shout praise in his courts.[2]

I must say a bit more about this last point. Hebrew man did think that he would survive death and enter into another world of experience, which he called Sheol, the place where the dead go. But it seemed a deep and dimly lit place, a silent place where the shadows of men remembered how it was to be alive. For a long time, it appears, the Hebrew concept of the afterlife did not take matters beyond that. Theological speculation in the last centuries before Christ, controlled to a degree by the teaching of Scripture, prepared the way for Paul's assertion that what has happened in the resurrection of Jesus will one day happen to the clay man. He will enter a new world of experience called the resurrection of the body. In this new world, his body will somehow be continuous with the body of clay, and yet sufficiently different that it will belong to another order of being.[3] But from the standpoint of the psalmists, all that is yet to be revealed.[4]

As far as the psalmist knows, this life of clay is his only time to taste gladness before he departs and is no more.[5] That is why he values long life, since if he is ever to achieve his aspirations, he must have sufficient time on earth. The wise and good man, therefore, "loves life and desires to see many good days."[6] God recognizes this desire and says of the faithful man, "With long life will I satisfy him."[7] Conversely, if justice is served, the wicked will not even reach midlife: "bloodthirsty and deceitful men will not live out half their days"—and the faithful man adds in the same breath, "But as for me, I trust in you," that is, he will trust God to give him a long life.[8] Thus, a man pleading with God to fulfill his promise will prudently add, "Remember how fleeting is my life."[9] That is, the Lord had better fulfill his promise quickly, for human life is measured in years, not centuries, and at best, it only "flourishes like a flower of the field; the wind blows over it and it is gone, and its place remembers it no more."[10]

Man in the Psalms lives perpetually with the idea, "Now is my only chance." If there is to be contentment, it must be found under the vine and the fig tree. If there is to be health and well-being, it must come quickly, before the feebleness of age makes one as good as dead. If one is to be vindicated from one's enemies, their teeth must be shattered *now*, while they still live. Justice and vindication must be accomplished speedily or not at all.

LIVING IN THE SHORT RUN

When one has little or no concept of an afterlife, how does one choose to live in the face of mortality? This question confronted the psalmists and many others in the ancient world, and it confronts us anew in our own world.

One of the more widespread solutions is to abandon grandiose ideas of leaving one's mark on the world or achieving superhuman status in this life. Be happy to live a good, solid life on a human scale. Do good work. Enjoy the pleasures of family and friends. Enjoy the beauty of art and the natural world. Carve out your small and temporary space in the larger human story, knowing that the story will continue after you and will be affected—even if only in a modest degree—by your having been here and by your being remembered by the few who knew you. Above all, be grateful for even the fleeting gift of life, lived, as it is, in the shadow of mortality.

This view of life in the short run is widespread, and we find it everywhere. It is lived out in the day-to-day choices of millions of men and women, and it is given artistic expression in films and music and novels and poetry. Stephen Crane asks only that "thou and thy white arms were there, / And the fall to doom a long way." E. B. White speaks of the passing seasons and the cycle of life and says, "All these sights and sounds and smells will be yours to enjoy…this lovely world, these precious days." Long ago the Latin poet Horace advised, "Since time is short, cut off long-reaching hopes. Even as we speak, life has fled invidiously away. Seize today! Catch it on the wing! Do not count too heavily on tomorrow." And long before Horace, Babylonian wisdom taught the same: "Let thy garments be sparkling fresh, thy head be washed... Pay heed to the little one that holds on to thy hand, let thy spouse delight in thy bosom! For this is the task of mankind!"[11]

The short-run solution is a summons to soak up life's daily pleasures: food and drink, the comfortable feel of clean clothes on a clean body, the touch of a small hand reaching up to a large hand, and the companionship of people who love you. It is a counsel to welcome each moment for what it offers and to live like the dragonfly, which "leaves its shell that its face might but glance at the face of the sun."[12]

It strikes me that, as a practical solution, this makes good sense, and I can say, to a point, "Yes, I can live like that." After all, this *is* our only chance at *this* life. Living in the short run will carry us at least partway along in our hopes for a happy life in a world where neither happiness nor life is guaranteed. And it is not altogether incompatible with the religious life. There is at least a strand of it in the Bible. The Old Testament places a high value on long life and happy children. The book of Ecclesiastes speaks of delight in food and drink, in home and hearth, in sparkling garments and a well-groomed head.[13]

In the months following Elizabeth's death, the realization gradually dawned that one of life's secrets was to be alive while you are alive. Life in the short run became a matter of finding something each day in which to delight. It might be the sudden, unexpected breeze that lifted a swirl of leaves about my feet. Or a sign that read, "Free eye examination. Buy one pair, get one free." Or an April redbud tree next to a newly green willow next to a dark and ancient cedar. Or a sudden bear hug from my son or an impulsive kiss from my daughter. I learned—or rather, began to learn—that contentment is a matter of receiving each unique opportunity for delight.

I began also to learn that it is a matter of receiving ordinary opportunities, too. The daily repetitive tasks can become opportunities for delight, if one can only seize them with love and not resentment. I began to notice that I liked rising in the morning and opening shades and blinds to welcome the day, rainy or fair. I liked washing the dishes, loving each glass and plate and spoon as I dried it and put it away. I liked parking in the schoolyard a few minutes early, soaking up the dreamy, buzzing quietness, listening to distant voices and birdsong and the slow swish of tires on pavement, then the bell and the sudden shouts and the wave of moving arms and legs and tossing heads. I liked reading to my children at bedtime, books that gave us pictures inside our heads and became part of our shared experience. I liked pulling up the covers at night and laying my cheek on the cool, smooth pillow. I listened to the barking of distant dogs and thought of Lake Maggiore or Cades Cove or Somewhere until sleep came. And at the present moment I tell myself that if I am to find contentment at all in this life—my only chance at this life—I must find it in this precise instant while writing these words in this composition book, seated at my desk beside an open window while a hushing rain falls and traffic moves along the wet street. This is the only authentic moment. This is the only moment that is ready for me. No other. If I cannot accept this moment with love and delight, then I have missed my chance, for there is no other.

But there is more to be said. The short-run solution can assume a worldview fundamentally different from that of ancient Israel and the Psalms. The psalmists knew the urgency of finding peace and exacting vengeance in the short run, and they felt pain and injustice with searing intensity. And yet at the same time, the psalmists affirmed an indomitable commitment to God. They possessed an unparalleled outlook on life lived in the face of mortality and amid pain and terror. Their practical solution went far beyond anything the short-run solution can offer, while at the same time supporting the human values assailed by injustice and death.

Because I, too, often feel that good must be achieved either speedily or never, the psalmists become my allies. But because I have a recalcitrant, willful spirit, the psalmists' unswerving commitment to God confronts me with a severe challenge. So severe is this challenge that it demands broader and deeper consideration. It is to this challenge that we turn next.

Chapter 4

THE CHOICE FOR PRAISE

Psalms of Rage and Terror

In the prison of his days,

Teach the free man how to praise.

—W. H. AUDEN, "In Memory of W. B. Yeats"

I grew up in a world full of psalms. When I was a boy, a small ceramic banner hanging on the living-room wall proclaimed these words from one of the psalms: "Delight thyself also in the LORD; and he shall give thee the desires of thine heart."[1] At Appleby Elementary School, every assembly program ended with the recitation of the last verse of the nineteenth psalm: "Let the words of my mouth, and the meditation of my heart, be acceptable in thy sight, O LORD, my strength, and my redeemer."[2] A counted cross-stitch that came some years ago as a Christmas present also bears a message from the Psalms: "Shew me thy ways, O LORD; teach me thy paths."[3]

We borrow words of consolation and encouragement from the Psalms, and that is good. But something has been overlooked. An element runs through the Psalms that we would not dream of nailing up on the living-room wall. I have never seen a decorative ceramic banner that reads, "Thou hast put me in the depths of the Pit, in the regions dark and deep." I have never seen a pewter serving dish bearing the inscription, "Because of my loud groaning my bones cleave to my flesh." I have never seen a Sunday-school button with this wish for the wicked: "Let them be like the snail which dissolves into slime." Nor do I ever expect to see them, even though these words, and many more like them, come straight from the Psalms.[4] The fierce psalms are in fact easier to find than the gentle ones, because there are so many more of them. They make up a major element in the Psalms for which *fierce* is exactly the right word. They give violent, unrestrained utterance to animal passion. From these psalms, we have the perfect right to borrow language expressive of our own pain, when pain threatens to overcome us.

SONGS OF RAGE AND TERROR

It has long been recognized that the psalms can be grouped into types. One of these types is the lament. In a typical lament, the speaker cries to the Lord for help, tells about his distress while protesting that it should not be happening to him, affirms his confidence that God will set things to right, and perhaps gives thanks in advance for God's help. The distresses that give rise to these laments are usually sickness or enemies and oftentimes both. The speaker is convinced that God's timely help is in order, and the reason he gives is at times pragmatic. If the Lord allows the psalmist to die, well, there is one less Israelite singing praises to him.[5] At other times the reason is legal. The psalmist is innocent, as the Lord can easily find out if he will only look into the man's heart.[6] The legal angle can sometimes sound like special pleading. The plaintiff complains that while he is sick his enemies mock him and grind their teeth at him. Yet when *they* were sick, he says, he fasted in sackcloth and went around as though he were in mourning for his own mother.[7]

It is frequently the case that the gentle verses that adorn plaques and collector's plates are the expressions of hope or trust, or the avowal of moral tractability, which also are a regular feature of the laments. The verse on your cross-stitch may indeed be from a lament—that is, from a psalm of rage and terror screamed into the wind.

I count 62 laments among the 150 psalms. You may arrive at a different tally because of the difficulty of deciding in some cases if a psalm qualifies as a lament. But the fact remains that the laments are by far the largest single category in the Psalter. Perhaps that is because we need more of them than we do the other kinds.

THE ICY WIND

Since I am a Christian, my own belief system includes elements not found in the Hebrew belief system. Now that Jesus Christ has come, I believe that somehow a new possibility has been achieved concerning man and what happens to him. I believe in the resurrection of the body on the last day and the eternal enjoyment of the presence of God—although I do maintain that we have been told less about all that than many people assume.

But even though my belief system is Christian, my experiences of life are more compatible with the ancient Hebrew belief system. In my own experience I have encountered neither the resurrection of the body nor the eternal bliss of the saints. I believe in those things, for they have been revealed through the coming of Jesus Christ. But the world that presents itself to my senses is the world of Hebrew man. And I find myself saying, "This is my only chance. The good must come now or not at all. How long, O Lord, before the good will come?"

To speak plainly. After Elizabeth's death, people told me that she was in a better place (which I could not doubt) and that someday the rest of us would join her. But that sentiment did not help at all. It was what I believed to be true, but not what I had just experienced. All I could think of was the terror and pain and rage and helplessness and despair and weakness and the icy blast and one final spasm of the hand, before death brought all to stillness and silence. It seemed to me that to speak of angels bearing her soul away was a trivialization of what she had just passed through. I did not want those images right then: I wanted the Psalms.

Nor do the dying always want words of eternal bliss and glory. My grandmother did not. I did not understand it then. I was only a little boy. But I understand it now. For some reason, I was alone with her in her room, not many months before she died. She was sitting up in bed, leaning against pillows, with a filmy bed jacket wrapped about her. She looked at me and said, "I am going to die." She was angry.

I said, "No, you're not."

She grew angrier. "I am too!"

I replied with a sentiment that was not my own, but which I had heard from other people: "No Christian ever dies."

"No Christian ever dies!" she cried. "Yes, they do! Just look at how full the graveyards are. How do you think those people got there?"

"That's not what I mean," I said.

"Well, what do you mean?"

The sentiment I was appealing to went something like this: "No Christian ever dies absolutely, never goes out of existence. Think of the afterlife, think of the resurrection." But I was too little to argue theology. She was a great deal older than I, she was angry, and she was my grandmother.

"Oh, you know," I said, and I let the matter drop.

She sat upright, fixing a steady gaze upon me. She had triumphed. She was going to die.

What I understand now is that my grandmother was balancing on the

Christian paradox, caught in the polarity between belief and experience. She wanted someone who could admit what she was experiencing. I turned out not to be that person. She did not forsake her Christian beliefs. She acknowledged that they were anchored in concrete realities. But she was standing on a threshold, leaning into the icy wind that was blowing to her from the dark and hooded future, and she felt fear and pain and rage. She wanted to acknowledge that those things *also* were real.

I find the same polarity in the death of Augustine, the great fifth-century theologian. He lay dying in the city of Hippo in the summer of A.D. 430. His friend and biographer Possidius tells us that Augustine had "those Psalms of David which are specially penitential" pinned to the wall next to his bed. "When he was very weak, [he] used to lie in bed facing the wall where the sheets of paper were put up, gazing at them and reading them, and copiously and continuously weeping as he read." Possidius understood this as "the duty of doing fitting and adequate penance before departing from this life."[8] Possidius knew Augustine well, and if he says that was Augustine's purpose in meditating on these psalms, I do not dispute it. Augustine did have a bad conscience and, without question, would have wanted to be contrite at death. But was there more?

If these were indeed the traditional seven penitential psalms, then we can look them up and read the very words that Augustine kept before him in his last illness. We find, of course, words of confession: "I acknowledged my sin to you and did not cover up my iniquity."[9] "I confess my iniquity; I am troubled by my sin."[10] "I know my transgressions, and my sin is always before me."[11] But we find more. Mixed in with the groanings of conscience, we come across the groanings of illness and fear:

I am worn out from groaning;
    all night long I flood my bed with weeping
    and drench my couch with tears.

My eyes grow weak with sorrow;

they fail because of all my foes.[12]

My back is filled with searing pain;

there is no health in my body.

I am feeble and utterly crushed;

I groan in anguish of heart.[13]

For my days vanish like smoke;

my bones burn like glowing embers.

My heart is blighted and withered like grass;

I forget to eat my food.

Because of my loud groaning

I am reduced to skin and bones.

I am like a desert owl,

like an owl among the ruins.

I lie awake; I have become

like a bird alone on a roof.[14]

These words give us a fuller picture of the dying man's experience. He gazes at the wall, moving his lips and weeping, for he wants words begging forgiveness for his sins. And he finds also a voice for his illness and pain and nearness to death.

The psalmist is our man when we need someone to acknowledge the rage and terror that are a part of living and dying, when we need the companionship of someone whose world seems like ours: passing away, running out, gone before the good comes.

You will have guessed by now that during the family crisis of which I have told you a little, the gentle verses never helped me. Desires of our hearts indeed! That was the very thing that was *not* coming true. Halfway through my wife's only chance at this world, the clock running, nothing getting better and most things getting worse, we were supposed to be consoled by talk about God giving the desires of the heart? Not likely! Not when every experience said just the opposite.

I found that sometimes what we need most is not nice words, but words of rage and terror. The fierce psalms give us those words.

WHEN WISDOM FAILS

And not only words. I said earlier that the psalms confront me with a severe challenge. Now it is time to say more about that.

Alongside the solution of the short run, in its ancient or modern form, we have the solution of the Psalms. The question is the same: how to live and suffer in the face of mortality. Some of the assumptions are the same: There is little consciousness of a world of experience beyond the present one; the good must come now or never; and the universe sorely offends against human values. Even part of the solution is the same. The short-run solution is to take the moment's pleasures and be content with one's mortality. This wisdom can be accommodated to the religious life, and I have learned from it.

But there is a point at which the wisdom of the short run breaks down. The present moment may offer no pleasures. It may become only something to be endured. It may at times seem a narrow passage through which one must squeeze, shutting one's eyes tight, suffocating, feeling one's ears and hair and skin being torn away, not knowing when the passage will end, but hoping against all hope to break through again one day into sunlight and air and freedom. At such moments the wisdom of the short run fails. The only adequate solution is one that does not break down at the very point when we need it most.

The psalmists offer such a solution. But it is hard.

THE GOD OF THE PSALMS

The psalmists' solution rests upon a fundamental fact of biblical religion: God is one, and besides him there is no other. This is, however, more than simply to affirm the numerical singularity of God, as if when you had counted him, you had only got to one (although there *is* only one of him, and that is an important fact to know). The faith of the psalmists affirms that Yahweh is the one God in heaven above and on earth below, and there is no other.[15]

Thus the psalmist cries, "What god is so great as our God?" and declares that "all the gods of the nations are idols, but the LORD made the heavens."[16] Yahweh is "the great King over all the earth," and he "reigns over the nations."[17] He is the Creator of the sea and the dry land.[18] His appearing is seen in the events of nature: in cloud, storm, and lightning.[19] Yahweh is the righteous judge of all the peoples of the earth.[20] His throne is in heaven, and the heavenly beings praise him; they exist to do his bidding.[21]

Yahweh was conceived as Israel's warrior, for he was mighty to save; as judge, for he acted with justice and mercy; and as king, for he ruled the earth and its people. He was continually said to be holy, "separate," for besides the created universe, there was only one other reality, and that was Yahweh. He was I AM WHO I AM; as we would say, he was the pure, unconditioned being who brought all else into being. He is "the high and lofty One," the prophet Isaiah says, who lives "in a high and holy place," and yet also lives with the low and humble, "with him who is contrite and lowly in spirit."[22]

Within this frame of reference, when the psalmists experience deliverance from harm, it is naturally to God that they raise their thanksgiving. He is their rock, their shield, their redeemer, their "refuge and strength," their "ever-present help in trouble."[23] Because God has been "a strong fortress to save,"[24] they raise their celebration; they "rejoice in the LORD" and "shout for joy."[25] They praise him with a "new song," and they tell everyone the "glad news" of their deliverance.[26]

And when there is no deliverance—what then? Sooner or later one gets around to wondering where God comes in when there is illness with no cure, wound with no healing, trouble with no release. It is a challenge to one's understanding as well as to one's faith when the Redeemer does not redeem. And yet the psalmists pray on, including among their petitions the cry, "How long?"[27] "I say to God my Rock," says one for whom God is still his strength, "Why have you forgotten me?"[28] "You are God my stronghold," says another for whom God is still refuge, "Why have you rejected me?"[29] Yet another wonders if God will act or reveal his presence ever again:

Will the Lord reject forever?
> Will he never show his favor again?
Has his unfailing love vanished forever?
> Has his promise failed for all time?
Has God forgotten to be merciful?
> Has he in anger withheld his compassion?[30]

THE MYSTERY OF MONOTHEISM

God's delays are bad enough, but there is worse to come. In a world created by the just and equitable God, the God in whom is pure goodness and rightness, where and what is the cause of our suffering? Granting that bad things must have a cause, their cause must lie in either creature or Creator. Very well. Then let us ascribe evil to the creature. After all, much of the world's suffering is caused by humans to themselves or to others. The psalmists are quick to recognize this. Many of the laments mention the psalmist's enemies, who are happy at his distress and do what they can to increase it,[31] and occasionally the psalmist confesses his own sinfulness as the source of his troubles.[32] Suffering in the Psalms thus has two causes. Wicked people choose the wrong and cause pain and suffering to others—and God allows them this freedom and permits suffering to result from it. Or people choose the wrong and bring pain and suffering upon themselves, and God allows and permits this, too—or even ensures it by seeing that people suffer the consequences of their bad choices.[33]

That is the way the world works, we say; that is the way the world is made. But now, you see, we are not far from a troubling question. Who made the world to work this way? Monotheism can give only one answer. If there is one Creator and all else is creature, then the power to choose evil and produce suffering was created by God. You must follow this all the way up. Place as many intermediary causes in the way as you like. Ultimately you must arrive at this: God is the Creator of the causes of our suffering and distress.

We are thrown thus quickly into the mysteries of monotheism. Indeed, the more strictly we adhere to it, the more severe our dilemma becomes. That part of the Hebrew Bible most passionately monotheistic—the book of Isaiah—serves us the mystery in its starkest terms. For there God declares, "I form the light, and create darkness: I make peace, and create evil: I the LORD do all these things."[34]

I do not like this at all. It is hard. Yet I can devise no means of softening it. We might seek an intellectual way out and say that evil is only permitted by God's provisional will. But we still have no answer as to why he provisionally permits it. We might say that evil is not a creation of God but rather that which God, by his creation, forbids. I want very much to agree—I think I *do* agree. But if so, it is still obvious that what God has forbidden, he has nonetheless allowed. We might say that there is some other power to blame for the evil and sorrow and suffering in the world—

some power that is beyond God's control and for which he cannot be held responsible. But you see already that that is the very path we cannot take. Nothing can be beyond the control of an omnipotent God. To be God at all, he must in the end bear the responsibility for everything that happens in the universe. Everything that happens, good or bad, is attributable ultimately to him, for there is no providence he does not send, no calamity he could not have prevented.

UNDER A RAIN OF ARROWS

We are left then within the mystery of monotheism, and within this mystery, the psalmists make their prayers. In their sorrow, they appeal to the only God they *can* appeal to, and he is the very God who either brought their sorrow upon them or delayed his deliverance while disaster fell.

"Your wrath lies heavily upon me," prays a voice from the depths of misery. "You have overwhelmed me with all your waves."[35] And again the same voice prays, "Your wrath has swept over me; your terrors have destroyed me."[36] The author of one psalm pleads, "Remove your scourge from me; I am overcome by the blow of your hand." And yet in the same psalm he says to God, "My hope is in you."[37] The author of another psalm cries out, "O LORD,…your arrows have pierced me." And yet in the same psalm he pleads, "Come quickly to help me, O Lord my Savior."[38] Old Testament scholar Artur Weiser comments that the psalmist "turns to God in the only hope that is still left to him that the hand which has inflicted the wound on him will also alone be able to heal it again."[39]

The psalmists groan under the hand of the Lord, and yet they groan and long for *him*. In all of the universe, they turn only to God. In the midst of their pain, they cry out that Yahweh is all they want or need. They need only to know him. "You are my Lord," they cry. "Apart from you I have no good thing."[40]

That is the psalmists' solution, and it shatters me to the center of my being. They see every present moment of this life in the short run, even moments of intense misery, as their only chance to know God, and the God whom they desire to know is the very God who bears ultimate responsibility for their misery. They do not focus on what *may* somehow come to be, but they focus on the presence of God in the here and now. "Whom have I in heaven but you?" the psalmist says, "And earth has nothing I desire besides you.... As for me, it is good to be near God."[41] "Let me live," the psalmist cries out to God, not so he might once again take up his simple domestic enjoyments, but "that I may praise you."[42] For him, the present is his moment, not merely to dress in clean linens and to put oil in his hair, but to love and praise God. He will seize every moment for God until there are no more. "I will praise you," he says, "as long as I live."[43] And all of this is said with little or no firm information about an afterlife. The present moment with its sorrows is not seized as a *preparation* for knowing God, but as the *chance* for knowing God.

I can hardly convey my feelings when I first understood this. I was washing up the breakfast dishes. Leonard Bernstein had just died, and the radio was playing a song of his. The words were like a psalm, and for the first time I heard what the words were saying:

I will sing His praises while I live
All of my days.[44]

I backed into a kitchen chair and sat in stunned silence, pressing my wet hands between my knees.

To turn in your misery to the God who is the source of all things, even ultimately of your misery, and not only to turn to him but also to praise him with all your might until your might has drained away. That is what the psalms call us to do. That is not the complete biblical solution, but it is the beginning point of any solution. The psalms do not alone supply all we need to strive on against the icy wind. But they do fill us with strength and power for the moment of turning.

Chapter 5

AGAINST THE WIND

The Faith of Job

Accept, accept that I have won, whispers the Devil. You can see for yourself that life is unjust, unfair, that suffering is ordinary. Who is stronger? I am, of course. Just despair, my dear, despair. Only tell me that I am strong, that Evil rules.

—SUZANNE MASSIE, *Journey*

On the whole, life is neither unrelieved tragedy nor unmingled happiness; it is mixed. Even on the morning of our family's darkest night, the darkness was not absolute.

John asked me, "What number do you want?"

"What do you mean?"

"We're going to play checkers."

"Give me number thirteen then."

He wrote the number thirteen on a piece of paper and taped it to my shirt. He pulled on a T-shirt with the number twenty-four in black marker on the back, and he put on a battered white football helmet. He had no helmet for me, but he insisted I wear a straw hat I had bought from an

Amish farmer. Checkers cannot be played without something on the head, and I think the Amish will agree.

John began the game. That is, he began the random movement of his red pieces across the board while I sat and witnessed the systematic removal of my black pieces. Had Adam, created in the full vigor of his understanding, watched John play checkers for the first time, he would have thought this is what checkers is: a game against which there is no defense. John's happiness at winning made me smile.

Then I drove to the hospital in the hushing rain and found Elizabeth crying because she could not remember where I was.

But not even for her was that day altogether darkness. Even in the fog of morphine and illness and fear of death, Elizabeth smiled. A nurse spoke to her, and she tried to sit up. Speaking to someone who was not there except in her own mind, she asked, "Who is it that's coming to the luncheon today? Oh, I know. He's a candidate." Satisfied that she had remembered, she smiled and lay down again. The nurse gave me a knowing look as she left the room. I knew exactly what Elizabeth was talking about. She was back in her social work days, when luncheons and political candidates and speeches provided comic relief from the daily stream of clients and crises. I was glad that, if she was to be a social worker again now, she could be one on a day when a politician was giving a speech.

I sat by her in my usual place, in a chair placed to the left of her bed, facing her. Her eyes were closed. In a moment she smiled and spoke again.

"I love you, too, Stephanie," she said.

ARCHETYPE OF SORROW AND FAITH

On any one day we are apt to experience both pain and pleasure. The one is sure to accompany the other, Socrates observed, as if pain and pleasure were quarreling children whose heads have been tied together. Because life is mixed, we can look for the good and usually find it, even amid the signs of our mortality and weakness. Our very resolve to embrace life's daily pleasures in spite of life's sorrows is proof enough that for most of our days we both can and must embrace them. And because life is mixed, faith must find a way to be constant, no matter what the days bring.

The first two chapters of the book of Job present a man who remains constant, even when his life is brought from the height of well-being to the depths of ruin. The book tells how the great man of the land of Uz—the wealthiest and most powerful of all the people of the East— loses his fortune, is bereft of his seven sons and three daughters, and is himself stricken with a terrible disease. Alongside the psalmists, Job is the archetypal upright man whose faith in God is tried by the power of evil.

The issue posed in the book of Job turns on the fact that Job is "blameless and upright; he feared God and shunned evil."[1] And yet this good man comes up against unexampled suffering. It happens like this:

One day the heavenly court convenes, and the "sons of God" present themselves before the Lord.[2] These celestial beings correspond to the courtiers who line up in any king's court to pay their respects and to report on their areas of responsibility. Among the courtiers is the unsavory character known as *ha-satan*. This is a Hebrew expression meaning "the accuser." Today, after nearly three thousand years of Jewish and Christian thought, a reader of Job is likely to see too much in this figure. Of course, the word *satan* is the designation used for this courtier, but it is a title, not yet a name. He is not yet the devil, not yet personified as a powerful spiritual being opposed to God and consumed with the desire to cause people pain and to make them sin. In the story of Job, the figure called *ha-satan* plays the role of a petty Near Eastern bureaucrat with the dubious function of spying on people and reporting their weaknesses.

The Accuser is just back from roaming the earth, and he has something to say about a certain Job, whom the Lord has held up as an exemplary servant of his. The Accuser suggests that Job's uprightness may well be a sham.

"Does Job fear God for nothing?" the Accuser says. "Have you not put a hedge around him?"—that is, to protect him from harm. "You have blessed the work of his hands, so that his flocks and herds are spread throughout the land"—that is, God has made Job quite rich. "But stretch out your hand and strike everything he has, and he will surely curse you to your face."[3]

Unfortunately for Job, it is simple enough to devise a means of testing the Accuser's assertion. The Lord gives the Accuser authority to do whatever he wants to Job's possessions and his sons and daughters, but he is not to harm Job's person. On the narrative level at least, Job's suffering is brought about to settle a dispute between the Lord and one of his courtiers. God takes it on almost as a bet; Job's reaction will either prove or disprove the Accuser's charges.

As it turns out, Job's reaction seems to disprove them. From the height of good fortune, Job is thrown into deepest suffering. His wealth is suddenly destroyed or stolen, and his seven sons and three daughters die in a windstorm. And yet Job remains loyal to God. He does "not sin by charging God with wrongdoing."[4] He does not curse God. Rather he declares, "The LORD gave, and the LORD has taken away; blessed be the name of the LORD."[5]

The next time the heavenly court convenes, the Lord points out to the Accuser that Job has persevered in his faithfulness. Nevertheless, the Accuser is not satisfied. "Skin for skin!" he cries. "A man will give all he has for his own life."[6] A supremely cynical viewpoint! Job still *lives,* and anyone will surrender anything—his livestock and the lives of his children—to save his own skin. According to the Accuser, therefore, Job has not yet endured the definitive test. "But stretch out your hand," he says to the Lord, "and strike his flesh and bones, and he will surely curse you to your face."[7]

"Very well," the Lord responds. "But you must spare his life."[8] So the Accuser is empowered to visit whatever torture on Job he can devise, short of death.

It is helpful at this point to understand one of the rudiments of Hebrew medical theory. Conventional wisdom had it that one's life or vitality—the *nephesh* for which the Accuser says anyone will trade anything—could be gradually reduced to the vanishing point. When it is utterly gone, the person is dead. When it is almost gone, but not quite, the person is desperately sick. That is what Job means when later in the book he says, "My life"—that is, my *nephesh*—"ebbs away."[9]

Obviously, the Accuser cannot very well say, "Let us kill Job outright and then see what he says!" But he can propose to bring his *nephesh,* his vitality, down to the vanishing point, and that will be near enough to death to measure the test results. A case of "painful sores" fills the bill, covering Job's body "from the soles of his feet to the top of his head."[10] The sores cause maximum misery while sparing Job's life.

The good man is accordingly struck with this disease, and he sits on an ash heap and scrapes himself with a bit of broken pottery. His wife unwittingly becomes an advocate for the Accuser when she counsels Job, "Curse God and die!"[11] Her solution is the exact opposite of the one we have seen in the book of Psalms. The psalmists view the depths of suffering as an opportunity to praise God. Job's wife, in sharp contrast, counsels him to use his last particle of vitality to revile the God whom he holds responsible. And yet Job persists in his former integrity. He replies, "Shall we accept good from God, and not trouble?" Even now, amid his suffering, Job trusts God, and "in all this, Job did not sin in what he said."[12]

The Sources of Sorrow

Of course, one might object, "*Job* suffered? It is clear that his sons and daughters suffered far more!"

I cannot help feeling the force of this objection. Granted, Job's children died, whereas Job was only sore. His life went on eventually in happiness and prosperity, whereas theirs did not. One might counter by suggesting that the dead, like Job, were blameless, and their undeserved deaths belong also to the general question of unmerited suffering. But it is also important to realize that Job suffers both by being smitten and by surviving. His story serves therefore to establish that people suffer all kinds of misfortune. You are justified in substituting any kind of suffering you like, including sorrow at the sorrows of others.

After all, much of the heartache in the world is empathic. We feel the hurts experienced by others as in our imaginations we put ourselves in their place. In my own case, I imagined myself to be Elizabeth, watching my children growing up as I was silently lifted away. I imagined myself inside a body wrecked by both disease and cure, a body that you have depended on for life, but which is becoming a vessel of death—and you cannot decide whether you have betrayed it or it has betrayed you. I imagined myself looking at familiar surroundings that did not matter anymore—the favorite wallpaper, the chair in which I rocked my children, the doll from childhood—things that now became nothing more than the room in which I lay dying. In imagination, I borrowed these realities from her and made them to some degree my own. Much of our sorrow is like that: the sorrow of the imagination, the sorrow of the survivor.

Because Job is both the survivor and the smitten, he becomes the symbol of us all. He becomes our Everyman. In Job's speeches later in the book, we find a constant passing to and fro from Job's particular case to the general condition of humankind. He may begin with himself, but sooner or later his theme becomes universal and includes kings, priests, princes, and nations.[13] The way is open for each reader of the book to become his own Job.

The question of faith can therefore be extended from "Shall I have faith in spite of my experience of suffering?" to "Shall I have faith in spite of what I know about the suffering of the world?" The second of these questions is the more severe of the two. Plenty of people at the height of their powers have chosen against faith and have given as their reason the extent of suffering in the world at large.

THE FAITH OF THE LORD, THE FAITH OF JOB

When we listen carefully to the story about Job, we find that, at bottom, it is a story about faith tested by the power of the void. That in itself is not surprising. What is surprising is that Job and God each trust the other, even when their reasons for trust have been severely reduced; and in each case their trust in the other is vindicated.

From the Accuser's point of view, Job's loyalty is bribed. What is praiseworthy about a person who worships the God who upholds his welfare? Perhaps nothing—especially if in the mixed course of life, the unyielding troubles come and faith is forsaken. What is discovered about Job is that troubles do come, and no ordinary troubles, but the worst that the Accuser can devise, and in spite of them, Job persists in his faith.

How many are able to follow Job, I have no way of knowing. I do know the feelings of nausea and incongruity that come when one prays in deepest misery and suspects almost to a moral certainty that there is no God. At such moments, God's seeming absence can become compelling evidence for atheism. That is the modern temptation, however. It would not have occurred to Job to doubt God's existence. But even in the modern world, few who are so tempted proceed all the way to atheism. It is quite enough to go only so far as practical atheism—to live as if there were no God. That is much nearer the Accuser's predicted response for Job.

Abdication of faith can take many forms. A woman loses her husband, and the stunning blow of loss immobilizes her so completely that much of her life simply shuts down, including her life of faith. A child loses a father and feels the almost instantaneous dissolution of religious belief. A young person in love with life and humanity encounters the sin and sorrow of the world—which God appears not to relieve—and decides that if anything is to be helped, we are on our own to do what is needed without God's assistance. We find it hard to attach blame to any of these responses. We understand them all too well, for we, too, are tempted to believe that virtually everything in our lives depends upon nothing more than conditions and circumstances.

Yet some do make the choice of Job. Parents of a child with Down syndrome see her as God's blessing for them. A young woman who has known nothing but poverty and illness tells everyone how kind God has been to her. Hospital chaplains see the choice of Job as often as anyone. People enduring more than the human spirit should be called upon to bear nonetheless speak of the mercies and goodness of God. Given the circumstances of our world, it is remarkable that anyone follows Job's example. That so many do is all the more startling.

Also startling is that God continues to trust *us*. He takes that risk. Presumably he could intervene at points where faith might be tested. He could prevent this or that disease, stop this country from waging war on that one, see to it that no child ever goes to bed hungry. Surely such intervention would increase faith on the earth.

But as soon as we say it, we see it is no good. We see that constant interference with the course of nature and with the exercise of human freedom might eliminate trials of faith—or most of them. But it would also make a world in which nothing important could depend upon the free good will and choice of either God or man. It would really be the world as described by the Accuser, in which no one serves God "for nothing."

In the world such as it is—and this is the point driven home by the story of Job's suffering—faith in God and the faithfulness of God are not matters of stimulus and response. Faith and faithfulness are unconditioned and unconditional. The presence or absence of faith is not linked to any efficient mechanism that reason can see. Neither Job nor God keeps accounts of each other, trusting the other only when certain conditions are met. The faith of Job and of countless people like him challenges the notion that everything depends upon conditions and circumstances. And that notion must be challenged. For our faith will never be free as long as it hangs upon the changing condition of the world, and our trustworthiness will never be secure until it can be depended upon even when the props are knocked from under it.

Beyond the story of Job's suffering, the book goes on for many chapters as Job and his friends argue the ways of God and the mystery of evil. To these chapters we must now turn. But when the dust of debate has settled, and the voices of Job and his friends have been brought to silence, we will have progressed no further than this: The pious servant trusts even the seemingly untrustworthy God, and God trusts the servant to remain loyal to him even when there is no longer reason to.

Chapter 6

THE UNRAVELING
OF REASON

Job and God in the Whirlwind

I would like to beg you, dear Sir, as well as I can, to have patience with
everything unresolved in your heart and to try to love *the questions themselves* as if they were locked rooms or books written in a very foreign
language. Don't search for the answers, which could not be given to you
now, because you would not be able to live them.

—RAINER MARIA RILKE, *Letters to a Young Poet*

It was some months after Elizabeth's death. I put on my jacket and
walked with our dog Dale through the short distance of woods. We
emerged from the trees and crossed an open area. We slowed our pace as
we approached the headstone. In the slanting rays of the October sun, I
took my place beside the rough rectangle of grass. A cold wind whipped
my clothing. Bits of weed from the nearby unmown field caught in the
red and white silk flowers. I felt the dampness of the earth through the
knees of my pants.

The most natural place for me was to the left of the little rectangle, where my chair would be if this were a hospital bed. I wanted to be at her side again, seeing that she had what she needed, that she was comfortable, that she lacked for no attention that I could give. I wanted her to be home when I got there, to answer my call when I stepped in the door. I wanted to talk to her about all that had happened.

I spoke softly to the ragged patch of grass while Dale gazed alertly around and snuffed at my ear.

DIALOGUE IN THE ASH HEAP

We had talked about it a great deal during the years of Elizabeth's illness. We sometimes managed to come to grips with the blunt, factual reality. But we never quite managed to answer one question: Why?

"Why is this happening to me?" she would ask. "You are the one who is supposed to know."

It was of course an important question. Why, indeed. And as a teacher of religion, I was expected to have some sort of answer.

"Is it because of something I did?" she would ask.

When something went wrong, it was sometimes her tendency—as it often is mine—to slip into self-blame. True, we do sometimes contribute to things going wrong: when we forget to turn off the faucet in the bathtub or when our foot is too slow in reaching the brake pedal or when we put the decimal point in the wrong place. Perhaps we contribute often enough in these ways—small ways, when you place them in cosmic perspective—that we naturally assume that we are responsible for things over which we in fact have no control.

I read of a woman who was a passenger on the ocean liner *Andrea Doria*. She went to her cabin and flipped the light switch at the same instant that the *Doria* collided with the Swedish vessel *Stockholm*. The great ship lurched amid the sound of grinding metal and the screams of passengers and crew. The woman flung open her door and cried out to the first person she saw that she had accidentally touched the emergency brake![1]

I understood the woman exactly. That would have been my immediate response too. It is my fault!

And so, Elizabeth would ask the questions. "Is this happening because I took the Pill? Is this caused by stress? What can I do to get rid of stress? Have I done something to deserve this? Am I being punished? What might I have done differently so this would not have happened? What am I supposed to learn from this? Is this being sent to teach me some deeper truth? Am I supposed to learn wisdom? patience? faith? I should have been a better person. I should have been stronger. If only I could think, I could find a way out. This is happening to me because of a flaw within myself, within my own body. It is my own fault."

These and other such questions we discussed, like Job and his friends, on the ash heap of our bewilderment and distress.

Our conversations were not unlike those found in the book of Job. The narrative we examined in the previous chapter brings the righteous sufferer to the verge of death and yet shows that he maintains an attitude of faith. At this point, we might expect another heavenly court scene in which the Lord has a few choice words to say to Job's accuser about his cynicism. Job has passed every test, and the Lord has demonstrated his servant's unconditional faith. The Accuser has lost the bet.

But the author has other plans. After Job takes up his position on the ash heap, we hear no more of the Accuser or his wager with the Lord. Rather, the story continues with the appearance of Job's friends. These persons and Job carry on a long dialogue in which the friends maintain that Job somehow *deserves* what has happened to him, and Job maintains that no, he does not.

THE REASONABLE WORLD OF THE FRIENDS

The speeches of Job's friends are premised on the belief that God is just and that he sees that people get what they deserve. The first speech of the friend Eliphaz is typical of the lot. He proposes that Job must be experiencing the results of his own bad deeds, for experience teaches that "those who plow evil and those who sow trouble reap it."[2] Since Job has manifestly reaped trouble, he must surely have plowed and sown it himself. Job had therefore better put himself in the hands of God, for "he thwarts the plans of the crafty," but "those who mourn are lifted to safety"; Job had better "not despise the discipline of the Almighty," for God "wounds, but he also binds up; he injures, but his hands also heal."[3]

I would never venture to give another person an explanation like that for their suffering. But I would leap at the chance to believe it about my own. To one who is already inclined to accept blame, the answer offered by Job's friends appears profoundly persuasive. When life is perplexing and I want an answer, when I must have an answer, when I cannot bear to live one more minute without an answer, then I am willing to listen to any answer that seems reasonable, and Job's friends are close at hand.

But there are two things wrong with the friends' explanation of Job's sufferings.

First, they are not really talking about the point at issue. On the surface, Job and his friends are concerned with the same events, but they end up talking about two different things. The friends are talking about deserved suffering or, at the very least, disciplinary suffering, whereas Job is talking about suffering, simple. The friends are talking about evil that can be rationally accounted for, while Job is talking about evil whose purpose or meaning is utterly beyond human understanding.

Second, the friends make the assumption that Job (and therefore the rest of us) has more influence over events than he really has. But really, what good is it to call Job to account when his shattering losses have been caused by marauders and wind and lightning! Job's friends of course realize this and do not accuse Job directly of slaying his children and covering his own body with sores. Rather, they add another link in the chain of causality: Job's behaviors cause *God* to cause the catastrophes.

We are not left to our own devices in deciding whether Job's friends are right or not. If we read to the end of this very long book, we hear a clear judgment from God. When all the speeches are over, the Lord says to Eliphaz, "I am angry with you and your two friends, because you have not spoken of me what is right, as my servant Job has."[4]

And yet in spite of this clear and unmistakable word, many of us are beguiled by the answer of the friends, for in their reasonable world, otherwise inexplicable sufferings make sense. We suffer things we cannot control. God can control them, *is* in fact controlling them. God sends bad things upon us because of our own badness, to punish or to improve us. Thus, the world makes sense.

THE PROTEST OF JOB

But Job cries out to God that he be heard, and with unyielding vehemence he rejects the reasonable explanation of his friends. Of their speech making he says, "Will your long-winded speeches never end?" and he calls his friends "worthless physicians" and "miserable comforters."[5]

Job is, however, in agreement with his friends up to a point. He, like they, attributes his calamities to God. Without exception, all the characters in the story, as the psalmists before them, admit that God is the ultimate source of Job's troubles—and no one for a moment attributes Job's plight to the Accuser. Again we face the issue in the starkest possible terms.

In global human experience, we face evil. God could prevent it. And yet he does not.

But why not? Elizabeth and I tried to understand this. Daily it crossed our minds, and almost daily we talked about it.

Ah! Perhaps, after all, it is intended to make us wise! But no. Although some people have lived with suffering and become wise—or patient or faithful or tender—we could imagine others and more easily imagine ourselves becoming bitter and cold and faithless. We battled the temptation to become those things, and not always successfully. We had to conclude, therefore, that when wisdom and faith and the rest arise, they must be a response to suffering rather than the reason for it.

At other times we thought that maybe we do, after all, bring it upon ourselves and upon other people. Here we made better headway. Without question, there are plenty of deficiencies on our part that go a long way in accounting for our suffering and the sufferings of others. Greed, injustice, cruelty, murder, war—the entire litany of things that we call "man's inhumanity to man"—these things do explain much of the world's misery and pain. We understand that a world in which people are free is also a world in which they are free to hurt one another. For even a good and all-powerful God cannot make a world in which humans are allowed free choice and in which the choice for evil is not also a very real—even expected—possibility.

But we found that not all evil can be accounted for as the result of humankind's folly. For even after one makes all due allowance for the competence of God and the foolishness of humanity, an irrational residue of evil remains that defies explanation, even when subjected to the considerable power of human reason. This, it seems to me, is the issue that the book of Job unrelentingly presses upon us. This is the issue that Job's friends think, wrongly, they have resolved. And this is the issue about which Job cries to God for resolution.

The speeches of Job bring us to an unbearable state of tension. Job affirms his own integrity, and at the same time, he affirms the goodness, justice, and power of God. Yet terrible things are happening, and the more we try to understand them, the more bewildered we become. One by one, all ways of escape are closed off, and we are forced to realize that evil simply happens in this world, that it is a quantity in the present universe, that it cannot be fully understood no matter how deeply one is able to follow rationality.

So we, like Job, wait to see what the Lord will answer.

TRUSTING THE UNTRUSTWORTHY GOD

The astonishing thing about the book of Job is that it brings us to this tension point and gives no answer. The Lord replies to Job out of the whirlwind, and we hold one final, aching breath in hopes that he will unravel Job's bewilderment. But he does not. Instead, he unravels Job. Something happens to Job in the whirlwind. He comes away from the experience no longer railing against God. In place of his despair, he has acquired a new perspective from which to view all his living, thinking, and believing. In place of his bewilderment, he finds a wordless eloquence that is not yet comprehension, but is at least acceptance and peace. I admit that I do not so much read these things about Job in the text as feel them in my bones. But this is the response that the unraveling in the whirlwind seems to require.

God's answer to Job is not an answer at all. Rather, it is a torrent of questions showing that God knows deep mysteries and holds absolute power:

Where were you when I laid the earth's foundation?
Tell me, if you understand....

Have you ever given orders to the morning,
  or shown the dawn its place?…
Have you journeyed to the springs of the sea
  or walked in the recesses of the deep?
Have the gates of death been shown to you?
  Have you seen the gates of the shadow of death?…
Can you raise your voice to the clouds
  and cover yourself with a flood of water?…
Do you hunt the prey for the lioness
  and satisfy the hunger of the lions?…
Does the hawk take flight by your wisdom
  and spread his wings toward the south?[6]

That is merely a sampling. The torrent extends through four chapters. Over these questions stands the challenge, "Tell me, if you understand!" The challenge is already a clue that the purpose of the questions is to show how quickly human wisdom reaches its limits. The Lord in the whirlwind could well destroy Job with questions, but he does not. The questions are far beyond human abilities, but their tone is whimsical and benevolent. "The Lord is subtle," Albert Einstein remarked, "but he is not malicious."

On a first reading, some of the questions seem to call for factual knowledge that humans do not have, while others seem to point up human powerlessness over the world. But the questions do not merely challenge human scientific knowledge on the one hand and technical power on the other. Rather, they challenge human *wisdom,* a quality that in Hebrew thought joins knowing with doing. To know (and do) the wisdom of God beyond the borders of human wisdom is in fact to be God. The torrent of questions therefore leads to this: If Job can declare his understanding of these matters, wield the omnipotent power of God, and rule the earth, including the proud and wicked—if Job can assume the place of God, then God will acknowledge Job the victor.[7]

UP FROM THE ASHES

The whirlwind is Job's moment of turning. In it the Lord speaks and Job puts his hand over his mouth. By closing his mouth, he lays aside his words and his wisdom.[8] He lays aside, too, the words and wisdom of others in favor of what he has seen in the whirlwind: "My ears had heard of you but now my eyes have seen you."[9] He repents in dust and ashes,[10] and he sinks into the healing arms of God. The unraveling of Job in the whirlwind is the resolution of Job's crisis. It is not an explanation, not an answer on an intellectual level. Even though God speaks words to Job, the resolution consists not in words but in encounter, not in rationality but in unraveling.

When the words are ended and God has revealed himself in the whirlwind, the reasonable world of Job's friends is rejected, and even Job is not given a chance to be heard. God has neither justified himself to them nor given a rational answer to the problem of evil. Rather, he has revealed himself as the ineffable One, the alien and other, who nonetheless is trustworthy to save. Job's unraveling shows that human wisdom is soon out of its depth and cannot hope to penetrate to a reason behind evil and suffering. And yet, the wisdom of God is greater than the irrationality of evil. Even when we feel we are lost in the depths of the void, God can bring forth meaning and redemption. That is the mystery revealed in the whirlwind. That is what allows the believer to flee into the arms of the God who does nothing. That is what allows the wind that destroys also to heal.

In spite of all Job's demanding, his story does not uncover an explanation for the residue of irrational evil that we find in the world. Rather, it maintains in the face of all argument that such evil exists, and that it has happened to Job. Beyond that, human reason cannot penetrate.

Job's unraveling affirms that God reaches out toward the one who suffers and yet endures in faith. In that movement of recognition, the God who knows the universe's inscrutable secrets descends to us, reveals himself to us, and for a moment takes us into himself. In the whirlwind we catch a glimpse of the hidden mysteries of God. Only a glimpse. But a glimpse is all we can bear, and it is enough.

Like Job we, too, have our moments of unraveling when we strive with God in the night of our pain and sorrow. Our unravelings may occur on a smaller scale and may be nothing on the order of Job's magnificent vision. But if we allow them, even our small unravelings bring us nearer the birthing place of the healing wisdom of God. They show us that reality is not contained within the limits of our words or our reasoning. Beyond those limits reality looms large. Beyond those limits is this truth: The encounter between the God who destroys and the person who nonetheless trusts him is that which raises us from the ash heap.

And yet there is more to be said, for this truth reaches its ultimate expression when it throws itself facedown upon the earth in Gethsemane.

Chapter 7

THE GOD OF THICK DARKNESS

Jesus' Faith in Gethsemane and on the Cross

The only God who is trustworthy is the One who does not interfere to protect the pious but who is present in the thick of darkness, perhaps even as thick darkness.

—LEANDER KECK, *A Future for the Historical Jesus*

It was late and it was raining. Four years had passed since Elizabeth's death. Stephanie and John and I were driving home, and they were tired and hungry. They began to quarrel, then to cry, then to express the crushing misery and loneliness of life without a mother, and finally, to do all three of these things together. I had the interstate traffic to contend with, and my glasses were fogging up, and the windshield was fogged from all the crying, and I was trying to stay on the road and touch the child in the front seat as well as the child in the backseat and steer and work the windshield wipers and take my glasses off and put them on and try to think of something to do and think of what to say. But I was only able to think one thing: *I cannot do this. It is beyond me. I cannot do this.*

At times like that, it is easy to acknowledge one's limits. I knew there were things I could not do and things I did not know and things that I alone could not give my children. I knew, too, that it was not simply a matter of hauling some woman—any woman—into the house to be a mother to them. It was impossible that they have a mother ever again. But surely, I thought, even in the face of that dreadful lack, life might provide them with more of what every child needs and what I alone could not give them.

The thought sometimes took the form of prayer. It was not a wicked prayer. It was asked in all innocence—or at least in what passes for innocence among wicked men. It was a prayer no longer to be the only grownup in the family, no longer to be alone in either the gravity or levity of our life together. It was the desire for a second toothbrush by the sink, for the sound of someone singing in the next room, for fuller participation in the mysteries of human life.

That night on the interstate, I felt beyond question or doubt that God was doing absolutely nothing about any of this.

Home again in my room, after the children were asleep and the house was quiet and the door was closed, I prayed a new prayer. "Dear God," I said—almost, but not quite, in despair—"grant the heart's desire. And if not that, then please, dear God, grant a prayer of your own choosing."

The moment I said it, almost in the same instant with saying it, I knew that that was what God already had done. He had not granted my prayer; he had granted *his*.

It was difficult to squeeze much comfort from that realization. But I went to sleep feeling that I had faced the will of the Infinite and, for the night at least, made peace with it.

There is much in the world with which we must make peace. Suffering without warrant. Evil that defies rational explanation and for which none is offered. The seeming passivity or, worse, malevolence of God. Making peace with all this is one of the challenges of faith. The psalmists gave their solution: Amid illness and trouble, and with little notion of an afterlife, seize the present moment to know God. Job gave his: In the depths of sorrow, trust God even when God seems untrustworthy. These solutions go far toward creating a place where we can trust in ultimate goodness in a world where there is sometimes little reason to trust.

But does anything hard and concrete lie behind our trust? Viewed from the outside, trust may appear entirely subjective and internal. Splendid that people facing extinction hold their heads up and affirm the meaning of life! But does anything in the universe support and vindicate our trust?

JESUS AND THE VERY STORY

The hard reality behind religious faith is the Very Story confronting the storylessness of the void. In a universe that often seems bent against us, that is full of terrors and dangers, that leaves us desolate and lost, we are nonetheless never far from this story. In it we find support for human values and hopes and strivings. We find a creative power opposed to the power of evil. We find meaning opposed to randomness.

We have already seen the story in the psalmists' astonishing laments: "Your arrows have pierced me—O Lord my Savior!" [1] It is the fundamental experience described in the book of Job. The wind was destruction and tragedy, and the wind was the healing self-revelation of God. The story is found, too, in our own turning points that lead us upward from sorrow to blessedness. Finally, it is found full scale in the work of Jesus Christ, and in him it attains its ultimate power. For his is the one true story, and it can become our story as well.

In Christ, God entered the noise, smoke, and bother of human life, took upon himself our bewilderment and pain and our heart's deepest longings, and showed us that time, the universe, and existence can be trusted, for *he* trusted them. The story of Christ—the Very Story—shows us that the infinite God wants to lift finite creatures to himself so that we can know and enjoy him forever, being placed for all time out of reach of the void.

The essential elements of the Very Story are a going down and a going up, a descent into the regions of the void and an ascent into the resurrection-life of God. This two-movement story of descent and ascent is the fundamental way Christians have understood the work of Jesus Christ.

One of the earliest accounts of the story is preserved in what appears to be an ancient hymn quoted by the apostle Paul. In the words of the hymn, Christ was in the form of God and was equal to God. As we might say, before worlds were made, in the timelessness before time, God had within himself that which was revealed in Jesus Christ. But even though Christ possessed equality with God, he did not cling to it. He turned it loose, emptied himself, took the form of a servant, and was born into the humanity of our world. Thus, Jesus of Nazareth joined us in our life on the downhill slope. So profoundly did Christ identify himself with us that he bowed his head in death and descended to the lowest regions of human experience. From the depths God raised him up and exalted him to high position and gave him the name above every other name, the name *Lord*.[2]

The Gospels, too, tell a story of going down and going up. No sooner did the eternal Christ come down and become incarnate in Jesus than he was wrapped in swaddling clothes and laid in a feeding trough. He learned Aramaic in what the people of Jerusalem thought a rough and unsophisticated northern country dialect. He joined the common people in the temple and synagogue. He became an itinerant teacher and made both friends and enemies. Knowing the risks and dangers, he went resolutely to Jerusalem. He prayed for his life to be spared, but when the temple police came, he did not resist. He was scourged and humiliated, nailed up to a piece of wood until dead, and buried. He went down to the lowest depths and plunged into the blind, random meaninglessness of the void. This was his life on the downhill slope. And yet the working of God overcame the power that seeks to swallow human aspirations into the absurd and purposeless. The women who went to Jesus' tomb on Sunday morning found it empty, and they returned with the message that he was risen. His story had not ended in extinction; he had reached a point of turning, and by the power of God, he had been lifted out of the depths and raised again to life and blessedness.

RESURRECTION AND FAITH

Within weeks the early church was announcing the stupendous news about the Very Story. Now the working of God had revealed the upward ascent in the resurrection of Jesus, and this was nothing less than the vindication of faith.[3]

The Resurrection vindicated Israel's faith and Israel's God. The raising of Jesus completed and validated God's workings in Israel, and the God vindicated by the resurrection was the very God whom Israel had trusted—"The God of Abraham, Isaac and Jacob, the God of our fathers."[4] This meant, too, that he was the very God whom Job had trusted, the God of those who composed the laments found in the Psalms—every Israelite, indeed, who in terror and agony of spirit had cried to him for justice and help. His vindication was accordingly the vindication of the faithful of Israel as well. They did not live, suffer, and die stupidly. They lived and died trusting in the God who would one day raise the dead and bring their stories into union with the Very Story.

The Resurrection also vindicated Jesus' trust and Jesus' God. The God who stood by the cross silent and unseen showed his trustworthiness by raising from death the One who had trusted him. The One who had trusted and entered the darkness was the very One whom God raised and glorified as his Servant and Son. Jesus' entire life of faith was therefore vindicated by his raising. Not only was his body raised, but everything he ever was, did, or said—his whole human story on the downhill slope—was, by the Resurrection, lifted up into the eternal presence of God and given purpose and meaning. The resurrection of Jesus verified that thus is life to be lived, trusting God even in the wind and darkness of his apparent absence.

Since we live on the descending side of the story, our primary interest concerns faith on the downhill slope. Days do come upon us—pray God they are few!—when we are overwhelmed by loss, fear, and desolation, and we feel ourselves plunging headlong into the random nothingness of the void. What does the Very Story say to us at those times when our own pain and desolation cry out that God is not to be trusted?

One answer comes to us from Gethsemane, the olive grove where Jesus wrestled with God in the night and yet trusted him whose way led straight through suffering and death. A second comes from the Cross, where Jesus borrowed language from the Psalms to express his faith in the God who had forsaken him in his hour of deepest need.

FAITH IN GETHSEMANE

On the Thursday night when he had celebrated his final Passover with his followers, Jesus left Jerusalem and went to a garden on the Mount of Olives called Gethsemane. He summoned Peter, James, and John away from the other disciples, and in words reminiscent of the Psalms, he told them, "My soul is overwhelmed with sorrow to the point of death."[5] He moved a little farther into the garden, threw himself upon the ground, and prayed in distress and anguish.

In Gethsemane Jesus faced a choice between accepting God's will and seeking his own will. I first felt the impact of that choice while reading George Hedley's book *The Symbol of the Faith*.[6] Hedley was himself in Gethsemane one Thursday night before Good Friday, and he paced off the distance from the garden to the crest of the Mount of Olives. It was just ten minutes' rapid climb through the dark olive grove to the summit where one crosses over into the desolate and unpeopled badlands that rush down to the Jordan Valley. As the sun went down in the west, the Passover moon came up in the east and shone full on the white buildings of Jerusalem. Gethsemane, on the western slope of the hill, was left in darkness.

There, twenty centuries ago, Jesus met his greatest moral crisis. One of his followers had gone to betray him and to lead the temple police to where he was. Shortly, they would arrest him in the dark garden, away from the crowds who might have rallied to his defense during the day. Three—Peter, James, and John—came farther into the garden than the others, but in Jesus' dreadful moment of distress and need, they lay down and went to sleep. Across the Kidron Valley, torches could be seen coming from the city gate. It would be easy now, before Judas and the temple police arrived, while Peter, James, and John were sleeping, to slip away among the trees, scramble through the darkness to the summit, and disappear into the wilds where no one would find him, where no one would bother to look.

This was the setting in which Jesus accepted that he must walk the downhill slope to the end. He was hardly serene about it. When Mark says that Jesus was "deeply distressed and troubled," he describes a state as near emotional and physical collapse as one can readily imagine.[7] In this state, Jesus prayed, "Abba, Father.... Take this cup from me." In these words, Mark says, he asked that the "hour" might pass from him.[8] Jesus' prayer was not merely a plea not to die. It was a plea not to suffer the *hour* and die. The time of prayer at Gethsemane ends, and the hour of Jesus' suffering begins, when Judas comes and Jesus says to the three disciples, "The hour has come. Look, the Son of Man is betrayed into the hands of sinners."[9] Therefore, not merely death is meant, but the entire range of Jesus' sufferings. He prayed to be spared the whole series of miseries: the arrest, the trials, the mocking, the beatings, the crucifixion, the last despairing breath, the burial in the tomb. Three times Jesus prayed, and three times God did nothing.

The three prayers were a struggle through which, contrary to his own will, Jesus submitted to the will of God. In the gospel of Matthew, Jesus' first prayer is, "If it is possible, may this cup be taken from me." The second is, "If it is not possible for this cup to be taken away unless I drink it, may your will be done."[10] There is movement here: from "If it is possible" to "If it is not possible"; from "Yet not as I will" to "May your will be done." It is an astounding prayer, to say to the God who does nothing to avert catastrophe and ruin, "Your will be done." And yet Jesus not only said the words but lived them out. He remained in Gethsemane until Judas came, and he did not resist when he was taken away, ultimately to be crucified.

FAITH ON THE CROSS

We know that Jesus trusted God to the last, because on the cross he cried, "My God, my God, why have you forsaken me?"[11] Confronted with the all-but-overwhelming evidence for the absence of God and the irresistible power of the void, Jesus nonetheless turned to God in prayer.

Jesus' words of dereliction from the cross are taken from the Twenty-second Psalm, a lament that begins with cries of despair at God's inactivity and ends with the singing of God's praises in the temple courts. By citing the psalm's first verse, Jesus calls up all the rest of it, too, and makes the entire psalm his prayer. As soon as we begin to read it, we find ourselves right back among the psalmists who trusted God in spite of his delays and chose to praise him amid their sorrows and nearness to death.

My God, my God, why have you forsaken me?...

I cry out by day, but you do not answer....

In you our fathers put their trust;

    they trusted and you delivered them....

But I am a worm and not a man,

    scorned by men and despised by the people....

Yet you brought me out of the womb;

    you made me trust in you

    even at my mother's breast....

Do not be far from me,

    for trouble is near

    and there is no one to help....

You lay me in the dust of death....

A band of evil men has encircled me,

    they have pierced my hands and my feet...

They divide my garments among them

    and cast lots for my clothing....

O my Strength, come quickly to help me....

In the congregation I will praise you.

You who fear the LORD, praise him!...

For he has not despised or disdained

    the suffering of the afflicted one;

he has not hidden his face from him

    but has listened to his cry for help....

All the ends of the earth

    will remember and turn to the LORD.[12]

An ancient Hebrew prayer became Jesus' own prayer. With its words on his lips, the eternal Christ of God assumed solidarity with the human race and bowed his head in death.

OUR FAITH AND THE FAITH OF JESUS

Here is the crux of the Cross: Jesus trusted God even when God was silent and unseen. He hurled his sorrow and lament up to heaven and ended with the words, "Your will, not mine." Then he rose and walked boldly to his execution and descended to the void. God did not take the cup away, and Jesus submitted to unspeakable terrors and death.

Precisely because God did nothing and Jesus placed his faith in him, the faith of Jesus summons forth our own faith in times of descent.

The question for us is not, Can we follow Christ like that? It is, Can we follow a Christ like him? It is unlikely that we will ever trust with the power and intensity of Jesus' trust. It is enough that we pattern our faith on the faith of Jesus and in doing so become a part of the Very Story.

It may appear audacious for us to place our stories alongside the Very Story, and so it is. The very idea, that a man crying and fogging the windows of his car bears any resemblance to Jesus in Gethsemane! Or that a woman on her sickbed, drawing lines under words in the Psalms, bears any resemblance to Jesus crying to God from his cross!

And yet the resemblance *is* there. All of our bewilderment and pain on the downhill slope is a faint and uncertain outline laid against the master template. We are not wrong to see the resemblance, for the call to the Christian life is a call to make the Very Story our own, to go down and to go up. "If anyone would come after me," Jesus said, "he must deny himself and take up his cross and follow me."[13] To follow him is to trace the outline of our obedience against his obedience—and that outline descends to a cross.

Nor is our faith misplaced. The God who does nothing is the very God who can be trusted. The God who forsook Jesus on the cross is the very One who raised him from the dead and left for us that Sunday morning an empty tomb speaking hope in the eternal future of God.

Chapter 8

THE FUTURE OF HOPE

Faith and the Resurrection of Jesus

It is only the love of God, disclosed and enacted in Christ, that redeems
the human tragedy and makes it tolerable. No, more than tolerable.
Wonderful.

—ANGUS DUN

I have kept the Bible in which Elizabeth marked the verses in the Psalms
and Job and the New Testament. I have also kept the card that she had me
print for her and fasten to the bureau mirror. By turning her head she
could read these words:

And the God of all grace, who called you to his eternal glory in
Christ, after you have suffered a little while, will himself restore
you and make you strong, firm and steadfast.[1]

After you have suffered, you will be restored. After the terror of the
downhill plunge will come the moment of turning and the ascent from
darkness. Even though the present hour seems your only chance for life
and firmness—and horrible to feel it engulfed in wind and darkness!—

God's eternal present contains his ultimate creative act beyond your infirmity and pain.

We are assured of this promise through the resurrection of Christ. The empty tomb is more than an isolated datum belonging only to ancient history and standing forever alone. Rather, it belongs to a universal, future history. It is the first sign of a general resurrection one day to become the story of us all. God's possibilities are not exhausted by our temporal existence. Therefore we may hope.

GOD FROM A MACHINE?

In speaking of hope, I wish to avoid either cheapening the human plight or turning the resurrection of Jesus (and the general resurrection as well) into a theatrical expedient. In its crudest imaginable representation, the Resurrection might be turned into little more than a device for forcing a happy ending onto a sad story—as if a schoolchild might write, "Daddy lost both legs and our house burned down and all the topsoil blew off our farm and then a silver bird flew down with a magic pea in its mouth that gives us anything we want."

In ancient Greek drama, plays sometimes ended with a contrived solution like that one. A god appeared at the end of the story and, by his intervention, resolved otherwise insoluble complications. On stage Apollo's descent from Mount Olympus must have been magnificent, but from the wings you only saw an actor being lowered by something like a block and tackle. The term *deus ex machina* still survives in our literary language, and we use it to scoff at impossibly contrived happy endings. Does biblical faith come with us so far, only to leave us at last with this implausible "god from a machine"?

Truthfully, the ending of the book of Job comes perilously close. After losing his fortune, his children, and his own health, after thundering against

God and railing against his friends, after being reduced to silence by impenetrable mysteries—after all this, in the last eight verses of the book, Job is restored. God makes him twice as prosperous as before, re-instates him in his family, and blesses him again with seven sons and three daughters. Job lives to an immense age and dies "old and full of years."[2] We are tempted to object that if Job had lived in our world, he would have died in the last chapter still sitting on his ash heap. In what we call the "real world," we are left to trust and hope while the world remains as it is, a world in which there are no theatrical happy endings, but instead, an unvarying mixture of both delight and sorrow from start to finish.

What sort of God would he be anyway, this god from a machine who turns out happy endings? Would he be in any sense trustworthy? I remember friends who said, "We are praying for a miracle; we are praying for a cure." This was one month before the end. I appreciated what they were saying. Who would not wish for good in place of bad! Who would not wish for the god to be lowered onto the stage with his timely miracle! At the same time, I could not help wondering if such a god might not be heartlessly cruel, allowing people to writhe in pain, knowing all along that at the last moment he would work a trick, and all would be happy again. Could anyone in his right mind trust a god like that ever again?

I think now that my negative reaction was too severe. There are people who "received promises, stopped the mouths of lions, quenched raging fire, escaped the edge of the sword, won strength out of weakness,…received their dead by resurrection."[3] For such stories we must be glad. And yet faith has something to say, too, when there is no miracle and we must stride on into the wind.

Most of us, indeed, are called to take the harder way. For us, the God of our faith does not consist of a god from a machine. It consists of a God beside us, even in the darkness, and worthy of trust even when he abandons us (as it will seem) to the power of the void. It consists of a God who himself entered our darkness and shared our abandonment. The God of our faith does not enter our story only after we have descended through the terrors and emerged onto the happy upward slope. He travels, too, the entire line of our descent through sorrow and suffering. God is just as present and just as trustworthy in the downward movement as in the upward. That is why he is not an improbable god from a machine, but the true God who can be trusted. Nor is the Very Story an improbable story. We see it everywhere there is a deathlike descent followed by an ascent to renewed life. Its very commonness makes it entirely probable—almost predictable. Therefore we have grounds for hope.

THE HIDDEN WORK OF GOD

Jesus trusted God who did nothing, and his life ran out its course on the cross. No silver bird arrived with a magic pea. No unlikely god appeared from a machine. No last-hour miracle rescued him from suffering and death. And yet God raised Jesus from the dead. If the resurrection of Jesus was not an improbable contrivance, how *are* we to understand it?

It is worthwhile to begin by asking who the resurrection was *for*. Not for Jesus, I think. One can imagine that if God merely intended to take his Servant up again into his presence, he could have done it covertly. That any of this process was open and declared means that it was clearly for the benefit of someone besides Jesus.

Nor was the Resurrection itself seen by anyone. There was the empty tomb, but we have no eyewitness accounts of Jesus' coming out of it. There were certain post-Resurrection appearances, but no indication of passersby who casually got to take a look. Rather, the risen Jesus *appeared*. That is, he disclosed himself selectively to people who had been chosen. And he did so for a reason: to teach them, to explain things to them, to commission and empower them.[4] The Resurrection itself was hidden, whereas the risen Jesus was openly declared. As for the empty tomb—that could be seen by anyone.

Because of its hidden quality, the raising of Jesus defies visual representation. I do not mean that the Resurrection did not happen, but that it is difficult to visualize. The sixteenth-century painter Matthias Grünewald visualized it as well as anyone has, and yet he fell short. Grünewald created on one panel of the Isenheim Altar, now in Colmar, France, a depiction of the dead and dying Jesus so marvelous that it stuns visitors to silence. On another panel, he created an equally marvelous rendering of a luminous Jesus rising from the tomb and bathed in yellowish red phosphorescence. That is, it is marvelous artistically, but it doesn't ring true as theology. Not to me anyway. I looked from one panel to the other and was unable to discern any connection between the dying and the rising Jesus.

That may be my own fault as much as anything. None of us has experienced anything comparable to the Resurrection. Nor will we, until each of us makes that perpendicular ascent into the timelessness of God. Until then, we do not need to have seen it, or even to have formed a picture of it. We need only the declaration about the risen Jesus and the tomb that was empty.

Here is what is declared to us in the story of the empty tomb: that in the concrete reality of history, against all-but-overwhelming evidence that life is futile and hopeless, at a particular time and in a certain place, we have been given a small but sufficient witness that faith in God will be ultimately vindicated. For those who trust God as Jesus trusted, the future will be their validation. God is trustworthy, and he will ultimately bring the faithful through the depths to the upward ascent that is not only salvation from sin but also redemption from our sorrow and suffering.

Subtract for the moment the pleasures of life—those things in which we can take daily delight, the simple celebrations that can be received, nearly always, along with the sorrows. Think only of the descent to the depths: the gray, gravelly landscape leading down and down, now sliding under one's feet, the thunder of the earth opening up—Matthew Arnold's "grating roar of pebbles"[5]—and drawing one in. At last, silence reigns over the clatter, and the bits of shale bear no trace that one was ever there. That is human mortality before the advent of Christ, and that is the same mortality to which Christ submitted.

Now after the Resurrection there is one thing more. On the "naked shingles of the world" lies a new stone of a different kind. Crimson against gray, the stone is a sign from the future that there is an uphill slope, that one has gone there before us, and that others, too, who trust God as he trusted him will be raised from the depths of the void. That is the message of the empty tomb. The raising of Jesus speaks to us within a history that has not yet run out to its own Turning Point at the end of days. But his raising belongs already to that Turning Point and is given to us as a message speaking the future things of God.

THE PATTERN OF HOPE

I said earlier that the commonness of the pattern of descent and ascent is an argument for the truthfulness of the Very Story. The pattern of going down and going up, in fact, appears everywhere. Jesus found it in the mystery of life and growth: "I tell you the truth, unless a kernel of wheat falls to the ground and dies, it remains only a single seed. But if it dies, it produces many seeds."[6] Jesus applied the pattern directly to matters of life and faith, teaching that to lead a life that comes from God is to descend and serve;[7] to give is to receive and to be blessed;[8] to be last—child, servant —is to be great in the kingdom;[9] to lose one's life for God is to find it;[10] to mourn is to be comforted, to be meek is to inherit the earth, to be persecuted is to belong to the kingdom of God.[11] In all of these teachings, we see the pattern of going down and being lifted up.

The early church saw the pattern too: To die in repentance and bap-tism into death is to be raised to new life by the power of God;[12] to sub-mit to others in a spirit of mutual interdependence is to revere Christ and to do the will of God from the heart;[13] to be poor in the world is to be rich in faith and heirs of the kingdom;[14] to replicate in our dealings with others the pattern of the Christ who descended from God to servanthood is to have the mind of Christ.[15]

The descent side of the pattern is the story of human civilization. I do not mean that everything is necessarily destined to become more and more decadent in a linear descent (although a good case might be made that this is true). I mean only that no matter how good and decent humankind might become, it will always be limited by its frailty and impermanence. A nation or a culture will have its moment of grandeur, and then pass into history.

The descent side is also the story of each human being. No matter how splendid and beautiful individual lives might be, each life comes to an end, and from our vantage point, descends into the void. The oldest man who ever lived died at last.

And yet, even in a universal history that is at present on the downhill slope and has not yet arrived at its End Time and Turning Point, the Very Story is the exemplar of which fine lives and fine moments are copies. The life of faith, maintained even against irresistible evidence for the unending plummet into darkness, is a falling and a rising, and therefore is a retelling of the Very Story. It participates in the Very Story and is a part of it. This is why George MacDonald said that the Son of God "suffered unto the death, not that men might not suffer, but that their suffering might be like his."[16] By their response of faith, MacDonald believed, men's sufferings "lead them up to his perfection." This is why Martin Luther King Jr. said, "I have lived these last few years with the conviction that unearned suf-fering is redemptive." By his choice of faith, King found that he could "transform the suffering into a creative force."[17] These are but different ways of perceiving that our lives can become one with the Very Story and borrow its redemptive quality.

Our small moments of faith and insight participate in the Very Story too. To risk falling off the edge of our own limitations, to bare ourselves to the untamed and alien power of the natural order in nighttime sky and sunrise, to decide for praise and trust in a world such as ours, to descend into our mortality knowing that even there we are before the presence of God—all of these moments are copies of the Very Story and embrace not only a descent to humility or obedience but also an ascent toward the life of the holy. Every such moment of turning, no matter how low or commonplace, refracts the Very Story as every drop of dew refracts sun, sky, and earth. Look closely and it is there, small and fine. Each such moment brings with it the redemption of God.

THE REDEMPTION OF HOPE

So Elizabeth and I turned our heads and read the card on the bureau mirror and knew that even in all of this, hope may still survive—and not only *may.* We grew in the confidence that hope is supported and upheld by the Creator of time, the universe, and existence. Through our hope we knew that life and the indescribable sweetness and desire of human longing will ultimately be redeemed from the power and evil of the void.

It is the power of the Very Story to lift us from despair. When bad days come, we hope for better—and do not stupidly hope, but hope with confident assurance. When we enter darkness and death, we hope nevertheless for light and life.[18] We know that One has been here before us, trusting God at each step and finding at the Turning Point the validation and meaning of faith.

It is the power of the Very Story to triumph over sin, evil, the devil, decay, the absurd, and meaninglessness—everything that belongs to the void. At the point of turning, the perishable will be raised imperishable. Weakness will be transformed into strength. Dishonor into glory. Death into life. Sorrow into joy.[19]

It is the power of the Very Story to redeem us from futility. We know that our labor is not in vain, for in the Resurrection, all of our history, all of the people we are and have been, all of our pain, sorrow, and yearning is caught up and taken into the presence of God. Nothing is lost, nothing has gone for naught, nothing is in vain. In Christ, our strivings and sufferings are given validation and meaning, for our entire histories bring us into the presence of God. We ride the crest of the past through the icy wind of the present and into the dark and hooded future, knowing that God always has a future, and there he will complete his good work of creation.

Chapter 9

FINDING
YOUR WAY

Thoughts for the Journey

The journey is simple, and it is ready for anyone.

—DESIDERIUS ERASMUS

It has been a long journey since those nights and days when our world turned around and nothing remained as it was before. And yet we have come this far, Stephanie and John and I, and we want only to go forward, stepping each day into the unhappened future and meeting there the opportunities prepared for us by the past.

Before closing this book I would like to say something of a practical nature about what we have learned and how it is possible to find one's way through the dark times to a place of faith and wholeness. It is my wish for you that in your days on the downhill trend, your heart will turn in faith to the One who is there even when he seems not to be, and your thinking and doing will be infused with optimism and hope.

EMBRACE LIFE

Life contains much that is noble and elegant, much that is drab and distasteful, and much that is somewhere in between. Life is a vast mix, and we must embrace it all. It may seem that I am advising the impossible. But when we embrace it all in the presence of God, our experience of life becomes richer and deeper.

In his poem "Pied Beauty," Gerard Manley Hopkins celebrated the beauty of things that are multicolored and blotchy. "Glory be to God for dappled things," he wrote, for the light-and-dark patterns of nature and landscape, for things that are fickle and freckled, for things "swift, slow; sweet, sour; adazzle, dim."[1] Far from rejecting the slow in favor of the swift and the sour in favor of the sweet, Hopkins accepted them all as part of life's pattern. Only God's beauty is unmixed and past change. Our experience of life is neither all sweetness and light nor all darkness and despair. Faith responds to our mixed experience by embracing life in the praise of God. And although Hopkins does not directly say this, we might well conclude that to expect life's beauty to be unmixed is ultimately a form of idolatry; only God is pure delight.

Think of the tremendous variety of human experiences described in the book of Ecclesiastes.[2] There is not only a time to be born but also a time to die. Not only to plant but also to pluck up. To kill and to heal. To weep and to laugh. To mourn and to dance. To embrace and to refrain. To seek and to lose. From a merely human point of view, it sometimes seems pointless. If everything we build up is eventually broken down again and every good is opposed by its contrary evil, then "what does the worker gain from his toil?"[3] None, it appears—were it not for the God who has given himself to us in his commandments and who will "bring every deed into judgment…whether it is good or evil."[4]

The apostle Paul knew the mixed nature of life and responded to it in faith. He found that the ability to accept the mixed contents of life with contentment was a work of the Spirit of God. "I know what it is to be in need," he wrote, "and I know what it is to have plenty." And yet this did not come naturally to him; it was something he had to learn. "I have learned," he said, "to be content whatever the circumstances." For he wrote, "I have learned the secret of being content...whether well fed or hungry, whether living in plenty or in want." And here is the secret: "I can do everything through him who gives me strength."[5] When we, too, learn this secret, we will be well on our way to accepting life's hardships as well as its delights.

ACCEPT THE REALITY OF LOSS

One of the things we learn in this journey is that nothing is permanent but God. Everything else, no matter how durable it may seem to us, will eventually come to an end. The psalmist knew this when he wrote,

> In the beginning you laid the foundations of the earth,
>   and the heavens are the work of your hands.
> They will perish, but you remain;
>   they will all wear out like a garment.[6]

We begin learning this truth with the first toy that breaks, and we continue learning it as our favorite sneakers come unglued at last, as our first car turns over two hundred thousand miles and comes apart bolt by bolt, as the great tree that was our friend since youth falls to a storm in the night.

Sometimes we do not mind that things wear out and are used up.

When our clothes wear out, it means we get new ones. When I have filled up yet another composition book with my journal, I look forward to the cr-r-reak of opening a new one. I always think that the things I write in the new one will be better and happier and grander than the things I wrote in the old.

But some things cannot be replaced. When they are gone, they are gone for good, and if we liked those things—or loved those people—we feel the pain of loss. The greatest love the world has known—we knew it would last forever!—either by choice or circumstance comes at last to an end. The parents and aunts and uncles that were bigger than life in our childhood become normal size in our adulthood, and eventually they become infirm and are lost to us. If we can bear to look that far ahead, we realize that, ultimately, we will lose our beauty, our health, our strength, our furniture (when we retire to Florida), and at last our lives. If we believe the Bible (I do!), even the mighty universe will one day come to an end.

Looked at one way, human life and growth is a matter of losing the things that we have held precious. But looked at another way, life is a matter of finding old things replaced by new. When I drive past the house where I grew up, I think of the boy who used to live there, who took one last look around his empty room—and moved on, to another town, another house, another life. The pattern is found everywhere. The innocence of childhood is replaced by the savvy of adulthood. The beauty of youth is replaced by the beauty of age. The life of this world is replaced by the life of the world to come.

So, for beautiful things that are now lost, let us be grateful that we knew them at all. Let us thank God, the eternal, shining Present, that he let us borrow them for a time. That is the only way we could ever have known them.

LIVE IN THE PRESENT MOMENT

The reality of loss recalls us to the present moment. If nothing is permanent, if all things are temporary, if every person we love will sooner or later be lost to us (or we to them), then let us love them intensely in the present moment.

I made my first steps toward learning to do this when in college. One day one of my music professors set me an exercise. I was in his studio for a class—or rather, for a tutorial, as we met privately. We sat near the window, for he did not like fluorescent lights and never turned them on during the daytime. He said to me, "Listen. Clear everything out of your head and just listen. I want you to concentrate on hearing as many sounds as you can. I will do the same." At first I heard only the sound of voices down the hall. Then other sounds came: a bird outside the window, the hum of a fan, children's distant laughter. But my professor heard more—a typist downstairs, the slight creaking of our chairs, the ticking of my watch. When he named them, I could hear them too. I realized the immense pleasure he got out of hearing these simple things.

Since that day, I have repeated the exercise countless times and have tried to take in all that is possible of the present moment. Across the field a meadowlark sings. The late-afternoon light is suddenly golden. My little boy runs after his balsa-wood glider, lifting his arms high, thinking of neither past nor future, only of the glider and how far he can make it fly. My little girl walks in the leaves, her long hair golden in the sun and the orange leaves crisp on the ground.

Life is a gift from God, and this is how it comes into us. We absorb it in the present moment. And once absorbed, it becomes a part of us, a part of our past and a part of our future:

There was a child went forth every day,
And the first object he look'd upon, that object he
became,
And that object became part of him for the day or a
certain part of the day,
Or for many years or stretching cycles of years.[7]

The future can be many things, while the past can be merely what it was. Only the present is both pliable and firm at the same time. Only the present offers both freedom and certainty. Many things have changed since that moment in the darkness to this moment as I write. But one thing has not changed: The present is the only instant in all of time in which to find our way to life, wholeness, and gladness. It is in the present that the meadowlark sings and will sing, and is singing still.

LIVE WITHOUT ANSWERS

It is not necessary to understand before we can trust. The really significant issues bring us to this: faith seeking to understand.

Think of it like this. When God created the world, he brought forth order out of chaos. That is why goodness, beauty, truth, freedom, and justice can exist. We understand these things. Maybe we do not plumb their depths, but at least they do not raise insurmountable problems of philosophy or faith.

Evil, on the other hand, is chaos reasserting itself against the ordering of God. Evil is absurd, irrational, and inexplicable. Reason and coherence do not operate here. The wonder would be if we *could* understand evil, not that we cannot!

Therefore, our task is not to arrive at answers, but to press forward with our lives *without* all the answers. Our task is to decide to trust the next step. We do not know the future. But we know we are in the hands of the God who does.

FIND YOUR WORDS

Eighteen months before Elizabeth's death I began keeping a journal. I keep it still. If ever I have succeeded in constructing meaning from a life that has at times been chaotic and fragmented, it was only because I laid it out, concrete, in the form of words on paper. If you will do the same, I predict that you will be astonished at what you can learn from your own words.

I suggest three simple rules to follow in your journaling.

First, no one can read your journal unless you let them. This is the most important rule of all. Only by giving yourself complete privacy can you hope to tell the truth.

Second, you must never tear out a single page from your journal. To expose a feeling or an event to the threat of possible excision is to admit that some feelings are illegitimate and that some events should never have happened. I do not see how we can get very far if everything is subject to denial. So, once in, a thing must stay in.

Third, while you are writing, all laws of grammar, punctuation, and spelling are suspended. The main thing is to get words out onto the page, as many words as possible, without fussing and fretting about whether they are correct or proper or spelled according to the conventions of written English.

These rules will help your journal to fulfill its purpose. In journal writing, unrestrained by what people might think of us and unencumbered by external standards of propriety, we seek to tell the truth. When we work hard at truthfulness, an understanding grows up between us and our journal. We can tell our journal anything we think, anything we feel. It will listen to every word and understand every word. Our journal will never judge us or think less of us for what we write. It will never tell us what we should feel or believe. It will never require us to be paragons of virtue or pillars of strength. It will let us be weak and wrong. It will let us be four-year-olds rocking ourselves, wrapped in our own arms. Our journal will help us put thought into words so we will know, sometimes for the first time, what our thoughts are. It will make psalmists of us, composing laments in true Old Testament fashion, bringing our rage and bewilderment out into the light of God's presence. And in my own case, journal writing has done more: It has brought me alive in a way I have never been alive before.

Because our journals understand and accept us, we can let ourselves go and let our words rush unimpeded onto the page. Spontaneity and freedom are everything. We are not trying to write literature or essays for our friends to read. We are trying to go ever deeper into our world of feeling and experience until, at the very bottom, we reach our point of turning.

If we work hard at keeping a journal that is truthful and honest, we will find a lot of rubbish coming out. Depending on our mood at the moment and on our commitment to write down honestly whatever is inside us, we may find that the first words to come are words of anger, boredom, frustration, and tedium. It is a good thing, too, for we need some place to put them. We need to siphon them off and get rid of them. Writing them down is one way of making them concrete, so that we might expel them.

Underneath the poor words is the one place where I have found whatever good words there are. Not all is terrible in our journals. E. B. White, a longtime journal keeper, said his journals were "full of rubbish," but they occasionally managed "to report something in exquisite honesty and accuracy."[8] We need that too, and we are likely to discover that honesty and accuracy lie drowning beneath a sea of poor words, which are of course the first to tumble out. I have found that sometimes, at the end of a writing session, when I feel I can only write a little more before running out completely, good words come that I did not know were there, and something honest appears. In journal writing, honesty is the primary virtue, and accuracy the somewhat distant secondary one. Give me, please, honesty above all else! We can be accurate when honesty never enters into our heads. But if we are being honest—speaking the truth, neat and fine, small and up close—we are reaching for something far harder and far more important than mere accuracy. Moving out the poor words often uncovers something hidden—and that is worth getting to.

GIVE YOURSELF THE TIME YOU NEED

In my own dark days, someone said to me, "Many of your friends will not realize how long it takes. But you must give yourself the time you need." I came back to that thought again and again. It calmed me when I was impatient, and it helped me respect my own pace.

Your pace may be different from mine. Mine is rather slow. I like to watch baseball, because the plays in which something actually happens are spaced apart, and I have time to contemplate the beauty and elegance of the game. But I dislike watching ice hockey. It is too fast and frenetic; it gives me no time to think. When I can have my own way, life will be more like baseball.

One of your challenges will be to maintain a pace that is right for you, neither too fast nor too slow. Allow yourself to grow and change and unfold in a way that feels natural to you, while realizing that some moments of growth will feel like terrible leaps into risk and danger.

BE ALERT TO OPPORTUNITIES FOR GROWTH

Opportunities for growth are one of two things. They are sometimes moments of turning, in which it feels that we have reached some tiny place inside ourselves that suddenly opens up to something infinitely large. That is, we have met God. We have plunged over the dizzying precipice of our own limitations and fallen into his presence. At other times, opportunities for growth are moments of unraveling, in which it feels that something we believed before has dissolved and been replaced by a stronger and better thing. That is, we have met God in another way, and we have heard more clearly what he is saying to us.

I think opportunities for growth must lie all around us, and we may take the ones we need and the ones we are ready for. Each one comes as a gift. I can think of no way to force them to come. Our job is to maintain a stance of readiness—which we might do through prayer and Bible reading and worship and work—and when the moment comes, to take the now-or-never plunge that Robert Louis Stevenson described: the flinging of oneself forward "with that kind of anger of despair that has sometimes stood me in stead of courage."9

LEARN TO BE SELFISH IN THE RIGHT WAY

It was early January, just over a week after Elizabeth died. The social conventions were behind us, and the last bowl of potato salad was freezing in the back of the refrigerator. Emotions were still spinning, and the world had not put itself together again, quite. I realized that three people were looking to me to see they got what they needed: Stephanie and John made two, and I made the third. When the children needed food and baths and play and attention, it was up to me to see that they got them. When I needed rest and exercise and meaningful work, that was up to me too. It always had been, of course, but now the fact was thrown into stark relief. When I need hot food, I will cook it; when I need music, I will make it; when I need rest, I will put myself to bed.

I have called this "learning to be selfish," but it isn't really. It is only becoming sensible about one's needs, and when one is a parent of small children, about their needs, too.

Most of us succeed in furnishing ourselves with the requirements of biological life: food, rest, and washing. But we may find it more difficult to furnish ourselves with the requirements of the inner life: solitude, reflection, and prayerfulness. It is easier for me to wash socks than to write in my journal, to move objects in my house from one horizontal surface to another than to sit still and compose my inner space. Perhaps I have been taught that it is important to be productive, without being taught that stillness and solitude are also productive. They produce the inner life, without which we are only stomachs with legs.

GIVE YOURSELF SOLITUDE

Being alone in the right amount and in the right way is called solitude. Solitude is the Sabbath rest of the spirit. It is a time of relief from busyness. The virtue of solitude is that it gives us occasion to rest, to reflect, to pray, and to see the meaning in our lives.

Yes, that is its virtue, and that is also the very reason it is difficult for us. Relief from busyness does not always feel like relief; it sometimes feels like torment. Occasion to reflect is sometimes the very thing we want most to avoid. For as we reduce the noises coming in from the outside, our inner thoughts become audible, and we must face the very things we want to escape. A bereaved person will often say, cheerfully and with lifted chin, "Well, I'm keeping busy!" I hear this all the time. I fear that often it means, "I am swamping my senses with activity and sound and distraction. Peace and quiet are too painful to bear."

The trouble with "keeping busy" is that it can prevent us from doing the very thing we need to do most. When my inner life is in disarray, what it needs of course is attention. Chaos needs to be brought to order, at least to passable order; pandemonium needs to be brought to tranquillity, as best I can manage it. But when I retreat to a quiet place with no book and no radio, there I am, alone with the unhappy memory that comes again, the weakness I prefer not to think about, the fear that the future will be no better than the past—and the resentment that I have not had enough solitude! No wonder we prefer to keep busy. No wonder we pass over our inner life in a rush to get to the distractions.

But the distractions do not consistently work. I find that when my inner self needs solitude, it will have it one way or another. When with a group of friends, I might drop out of the conversation while my mind wanders to distant thoughts. When playing with the children, I might be pushing the swing while my inner self is roaming a million miles away. Stephanie would never let me get by with this. I would know I had been stealing solitude from her when, coming out of a fog, I would hear her saying, "Earth to Daddy! Earth to Daddy!"

When we are crushed with a terrible emotion, we must feel what there is to feel of it and then move on. If we move on without feeling it, it follows us when it might have been left behind. Unfelt feelings and unshed tears will sooner or later cause trouble. Better to have them out now than to accumulate them and then try to distract yourself from thinking about them. But again, the distractions do not really work, and my children would not put up with this either. I would know I was living with unresolved sorrow when Stephanie would prop up the corners of my mouth with her fingers and say, "Daddy! Smile! I don't want to live with a sad daddy."

In the life of the spirit, solitude is also the place where we talk with God. "When you pray," Jesus says, "go into a room by yourself, shut the door, and pray to your Father who is there in the secret place."[10] In solitude and hiddenness we say our prayers only for God, and there, in our private place, he meets us.

At some time during these years, I came across this prayer of Rabi'a of Basra:

O, my Lord, the stars are shining and the eyes of men are closed, and the kings have shut their doors, and every lover is alone with his beloved, and here I am alone with thee. O my Lord, if I worship thee from fear of hell, burn me in hell, and if I worship thee in hope of paradise, exclude me thence, but if I worship thee for thine own sake, then withhold not from me thine eternal beauty. [11]

I could make these words my own. Here was the prayer of a woman who prayed, as I did, in the solitude of the night and who communed with God, as I aspired to do, for God's own sake.

As I began to give my inner life the solitude it needed, I learned that our place of contentment, serenity, and joy is deep within our selves. I learned that serenity does not depend on anything exterior, that tranquillity and peace must be sought within. To say it bluntly, nothing and no one *out there* can make you happy. I learned, too, that our knowledge of God takes place at this inner point of certainty. He is *manifest* in the storm, in the breaking of bread, in Scripture; but he is *known* at the innermost place of our souls.

GIVE YOURSELF COMPANIONSHIP

Being together in the right amount and in the right way is called companionship, and like solitude, it is a great good. The virtue of companionship is that it gives us the context we need to play our part in the human drama. It gives us the opportunity to give and receive the affection by which C. S. Lewis accounted for "nine-tenths of whatever solid and durable happiness there is in our natural lives."[12] And it gives us the opportunity to work together for right relationships among people, that which the Bible calls justice and which is one of the hallmarks of the kingdom of God.

Many expressions of human life can only be acted out in company with others: playing Wiffle ball, running hand in hand over a grassy common, talking about things that matter, making each other laugh, making love. I cannot think of any way to do these things alone. People besides ourselves are the necessary context for expressing our full humanity. We have to have other people if we want to play checkers or toss a baseball or converse or dance. Our human life would be impoverished beyond enduring were it not for the fellowship of people we love and who love us.

Most of us make a distinction between acquaintances and friends, and a further distinction between friends and best friends. Of best friends we may have only a few, or only one. I believe that having a best friend makes us more thoroughly human than anything else this world has to offer.

"A friend," Aristotle said, "is another *you*."[13] He meant that friendship is the expression toward another person of the feelings that a good man must also feel for himself: the single-minded desire for the good, the wish that the other person not only be preserved but be preserved just as he is, the delight in conversation (for there are pleasant memories and fair hopes and an inexhaustible fund of topics), and the unstinting fellowship of joys and sorrows.

A similar idea is given whimsical expression in a tale found in the

Symposium of Plato.[14] Long ago, people were fastened to each other by twos, making a kind of binary person. These binary people were happy, for they never felt alone in the world. But a great tragedy happened. Out of fear, the gods split the binary people apart. Many of them never found their other selves ever again. But some did, and when they did, their happiness was unutterable. They confessed it as their heart's desire to be melted and welded together into one again, so they could live together always and even die together.

That is what it is like to find a friend who is another you. When such friends talk, ideas pass back and forth and are understood just as they are meant. Talk between such friends can go on and on, for they are always saying, in different ways, "Tell me more; always tell me more." They are letting more and more of themselves come out and more and more of the other person come in. Each is welcome, even in the unguarded corners of the heart, for between them is neither shame nor blame. Each is safe, for they will never willfully wrong each other. They are no longer separated, because now they have come together again after aeons of absence and bewilderment. That is the way it *feels* anyway to find such a friend: to come inside the other and to allow the other inside you; to invite and to be invited; to permit and to be permitted; to give and to receive; to understand and to be understood; to know and to be known; and at last, at long, long last, to be *one* with another person as it was meant to be in the time before time, before memory, before disorder and confusion violated the world.

I wish I could guarantee that a friend like that is easily found. Sadly, I cannot. And yet we can be vigilant and ready to welcome such a friend should God, in his mercies, send one to us. We can be ready to share our minds and to listen while our friend shares his. We can pour into our friendship the honesty, truthfulness, and courage that such friendship demands. When you develop such a friendship, cling to your friend with fierce loyalty. No treasure on earth will be more valuable.

Forming such a friendship will supply two needs at once: solitude and society. You can be in company with your friend without losing your solitude. It sounds ludicrous to say so, but being with your friend is as good as being alone. At the same time, your friend will free you to be yourself in human companionship. As this happens, you will find that you are becoming ennobled. Your friend will never ask you to be better than you are, but you will discover that because you have a friend, you are better than you were.

Knowing a best friend is an analogue for knowing God. In best friendship, you will discover something outside yourself that is larger than yourself (friends and lovers instinctively know this) and that has profound importance and meaning. Friendship at its best will help you know him who is your ultimate Other Self and your kindest Friend.

TRUST THE TRUSTWORTHY GOD

I do not know what your experience of God has been. At one time or another most of us peer over the edge of the molecular universe and feel that there is nothing else out there, that we are alone, that our prayers are mail posted to a nonexistent address.

Perhaps this has been your experience, too. I think, however, that most of us, most of the time, grant at the very least that, besides the molecular universe, there is an additional Something-or-other out there, and that life at its best will seek to participate not only in physical reality but in the life of the Something-or-other as well.

When I say that this Something is worthy of our trust, I am speaking at the most fundamental level of faith. Indeed, to say that God is trustworthy is the most important thing I can say about him. If times come upon you when that belief is the only one you can hold on to—as those times came upon me—it will be enough. Better times will come, when you will see more of him—or rather when he will disclose more of himself to you.

I believe that human wholeness cannot be achieved apart from the work of God, who makes possible our right standing with himself and with our fellow creatures. God came down into weakness, servitude, and death in the person of Jesus Christ, who went the way of the cross and, beyond the cross, was raised into the life that God alone gives. We become participants in this story—the one completely true story—when we throw aside our self-reliance and place our confidence in the trustworthy God. That is, the outline of our Christian life is a descent from pride and willfulness to self-denial, repentance, and obedience. This descent on our part is matched on God's part by the ascent into the new life of the Spirit as he forgives us, empowers us, and sets us to work in the church. The movement of descent and ascent is given liturgical form in baptism, as the apostle Paul indicates, for the old self is crucified and is buried, and the new is raised and given life.[15] A new context of trust and reconciliation is thus created by the power of the Very Story, and in company with others who have made the story their own, we begin to grow toward genuine humanity and wholeness.

We *begin* to grow, you must understand; we *begin* to make the Very Story our own. All of our life and faith in the present age is only a beginning. Some days, indeed, we will feel as if nothing has changed. Although renewed by the Spirit of God, we still have it all to face: tears as well as laughter, pain as well as pleasure, death as well as life. We will conduct our temporal lives always in the midpoint between heaven and earth, between promise and fulfillment, between this age and the age to come. We will live in the world, but not of the world.[16] We will grieve no less than others, but we will grieve now with hope.[17] We will suffer still, "as the sufferings of Christ flow over into our lives," but we will know God now as "the Father of compassion and the God of all comfort."[18] And we will know that in all of our life's moments, in the downward movement to sorrow as well as the upward movement to joy, we live in the presence of the God who is Lord of both sorrow and joy.

THE WIND THAT DESTROYS AND HEALS

The mind enters itself, and God the mind,

And one is One, free in the tearing wind.

—THEODORE ROETHKE, "In a Dark Time"

In our house hangs a shell collection. Elizabeth made it as a school pro-ject when she was in the eighth grade. It contains forty-nine kinds of shells—apple murex, turkey wing, calico scallop, jingle shell, lobed moon shell, common auger, common cockle, keyhole limpet—glued neatly in rows and labeled with common and scientific names.

When I look at these shells, I think of a time in the icy wind and thick darkness when I knew that God was near and that he stretched forth his hand not to smite, but to heal.

Our family took a trip at the end of Elizabeth's last summer. Before the opportunity was lost forever, she wanted to pack ourselves and the children into the car and travel to the beach to pick up shells.

We divided the travel there into two half-days. Friday afternoon we drove through fair weather, but Saturday morning through foul. Gray clouds piled up in the south, and they brought rain. We were quiet as we drove into the thickening clouds and darkness. The windshield wipers could never take the rain quite away.

We found a room in a motel across the road from the waterfront. We could see the beach from our upstairs window. But the weather had become almost frighteningly violent. The rain fell in sheets, and the wind pushed hard against us and drove the rain into our faces. We stayed indoors all that afternoon and evening and went to bed hoping that the morning would break fair.

Elizabeth awakened me in the middle of the night.

"When the wind blows," she said, "I can feel the bed shake."

Lightning showed trees bending and sea oats whipping hard against the ground. The sound of thunder, wind, and rain was deafening.

I switched on the television. The channels were dead. I looked out the window. A single vehicle moved down the street. I found my shoes with my bare feet and reached for my shirt.

"I'll go down and listen to the car radio," I said.

Blind in the wind and rain and darkness, I felt my way along the wooden staircase. The railing shook in my hands. Rain poured down my collar, and my wet shirt clung horribly to my skin. I crouched and ran to the car, cursing my hands as they clumsily worked the key. I jerked open the door and flung myself inside. The car shuddered in the wind.

No AM stations came in at all. Seven or eight FM stations pierced the storm with easy listening or New Age music or Alexander Scourby reading the book of Genesis—the part about Jacob wrestling with the man all night. I listened until an announcer said a tropical storm was centered sixty-five miles south of Bay St. Louis and was not expected to move in the next twenty-four hours.

The weather was not going to break, not tomorrow, not the next day.

We decided to leave for home as soon as it was light. Perhaps we could outrun the storm for at least part of our way.

Dawn came. We made breakfast and woke the children. While I packed the car, the others waited upstairs. Then they made their way down the shuddering stairway, clutching the rail and one another in the wind.

I looked at Elizabeth and knew that this was, for her, a good-bye.

"Turn right," she said. "Let's drive down the beach for one last look."

We drove slowly in the buffeting wind, past vacant lots covered with shivering sea oats, and past deserted beach houses. The car shook and lurched in the wind. Ponderous waves crashed against the shore.

"The storm must be washing up a lot of shells," Elizabeth said.

We came to the end of the road and to the last deserted house on the beach. I pulled into the drive, and we sat quietly for a moment, I leaning against the steering wheel and gazing out at the Gulf and the storm, she gazing too, the children leaning forward to watch the waves pound against the sand.

Elizabeth spoke quietly. "Let's get out and look for shells."

Four years before we never would have dreamed of doing that. Now we knew it was the only sensible thing. This was the reason we had come. I drove farther up the drive and stopped the car, and the four of us strode into the wind toward the beach.

The storm had driven plenty of shells ashore. But everything of any size had been shattered. The steep downslope of the beach was strewn with tiny fragments of pink, orange, and brown shell.

Elizabeth stooped and gathered up a few fragments, sorting them in the palm of her hand. "This one looks like a moon shell," she said, "and I think this must be part of a calico scallop."

She and the children picked at the bits of shell for a moment, selected a handful of small broken things, looked into the wind and shivered, and started slowly back to the car.

I walked alone to the edge of the beach. Waves exploded at my feet, bringing up great gouts of foam that the wind ripped to shreds and sent flying along the sand faster than my eye could follow. The wind snapped my clothes around me and drove the rain straight across the waves and into my face. The rain felt solid, and it stung like bits of glass.

For long minutes I stood in that spot. I leaned into the wind, felt the rain, saw the waves, heard the thundering water and the howling storm. I was engulfed by the power of the storm. I felt its power enter into me, and I wanted to enter into it, too, to stand there forever and feel its strength.

I looked behind me. The others had reached the car and were shrieking encouragement to each other as they struggled to climb in.

I turned to look at the sea once more. Then I turned and began to walk, and the wind in my back moved me on my way.

QUESTIONS FOR REFLECTION AND DISCUSSION

CHAPTER 1

The Meeting of Past and Future: Making Sense of Our Story

1. Look at the broad outline of your life. Does your story, like Jacob's, contain a time of crisis and distress followed by a time when your life is (or will be) significantly changed? How is your life different before and after the crisis? What opportunities for growth within yourself and service toward others can you find in these changes?

2. Compare and contrast the two prayers of Jacob in Genesis 28:20-22 and Genesis 32:9-12. Then compare them with prayers you have prayed yourself. What do you learn about your prayer life by making this comparison?

3. What life experiences can you name that tend to affirm human aspirations and the belief that the best things we strive for are noble, beautiful, and good? What experiences tend to deny the worth and importance of human values? Which set of experiences do you feel is more compelling?

4. Sören Kierkegaard observed in his journal that life can only be understood backward, but it must be lived forward. What significant events in your life have you understood with greater clarity after time has given you perspective on your past?

CHAPTER 2

At the Point of Turning: Finding Light in the Darkness

1. When I was preparing to move with my children to a new town and a new life, a friend told me to make two lists. "On one, list all the things you will miss. On the other, list the things you will not miss. It is okay both to miss some things and not to miss others." Think of a time of change in your life and name the things you missed and the things you did not.

2. Any time of transition can provide an opportunity to feel both loss for what is past and expectation for what is to come. You may feel varying degrees of sadness and expectation when you move from an old office to a new one, change jobs or career, send your child to school, change family relationships through marriage or divorce, or suffer the loss of someone you love. If you are in such a transition, in what ways do you feel loss for what is past? In what ways do you anticipate the future?

3. Think of a painful event in your life—not a recent event, but one that happened long enough ago that you feel some emotional distance. Can you think of good things that developed from the event? Was there renewed hope? increased faith? greater kindness, humility, and tenderness? Do you think the good things came as a result of the painful event or merely in its aftermath?

CHAPTER 3

In the Shadow of Mortality: Life and Death in the Psalms

1. My sister Jo admires the French people for their quality of life. She says, "It's as if everyone gets up in the morning and asks, 'What pleasant thing shall we do today?'" In what ways do you regularly experience and enjoy the simple and pleasant things God supplies each day?

2. Miguel Ruiz, in his book *The Four Agreements,* says that just the pleasure of breathing is enough for us to always be happy. Right now, at this present moment, what good thing can you find to appreciate and enjoy?

3. In times of sadness and grief, do you find it possible to praise God in spite of it all? When you cannot find that possibility within yourself, how can you provide yourself with encouragement from others who can praise God even in time of trouble?

CHAPTER 4

The Choice for Praise: Psalms of Rage and Terror

1. The seven penitential psalms are 6, 32, 38, 51, 102, 130, and 143. As you read these psalms, note how they depict the utter realism of the psalmist's situation. What passages from these psalms can you borrow and use to express your own feelings?

2. In times of trouble and heartache, in what ways do you feel the reality and nearness of God growing stronger within you? Or in what ways do you feel his reality becoming weaker and less significant for you?

3. Sometimes, during my own dark time, I attended worship not to express my own faith (which was often weak and

🐦 beleaguered), but because I knew that in church I would at least overhear the faith of others. When your own faith is weakening, what steps do you take to find hope and encouragement in the faith of others?

CHAPTER 5

Against the Wind: The Faith of Job

1. Describe a time when you have felt the sadness of the survivor or sorrow at the sorrow of others. Do you think God feels similar sorrow? What beliefs do you have about God that incline you to your answer?

2. Think of the mutual trust relationship that exists between you and God. What are the terms of the relationship? What does God trust you to do? What do you trust God to do?

3. In the trust relationship between you and God, who is taking the greater risk? Why?

CHAPTER 6

The Unraveling of Reason: Job and God in the Whirlwind

1. John G. Stackhouse Jr., in his book *Can God Be Trusted?* proposes the following thought experiment. Suppose the person you are engaged to appears open and truthful but occasionally leaves town for a few days and will not tell you why. On what basis can you decide whether to trust him and marry him? Now imagine a similar case with God. In most ways he appears benevolent and just, but some things he will not explain. On what basis can you decide whether to put your faith in him?

2. In what events of your life have you been forced by immediate circumstances to decide whether God was good or just or trustworthy? How did you decide?

CHAPTER 7

The God of Thick Darkness: Jesus' Faith in Gethsemane and on the Cross

1. In the previous chapter the question arose whether to trust God even in circumstances where his trustworthiness seemed in question. How does the resurrection of Christ contribute to your deciding the question?

2. How was Jesus' prayer in Gethsemane answered? How was it not answered? In what ways can his prayer be a model for your own praying? for your own decision whether to trust?

3. The call to follow Jesus is a call to follow him with our own crosses as well as to share in his resurrection-life. What aspects of your life of faith might be described as following with your cross?

CHAPTER 8

The Future of Hope: Faith and the Resurrection of Jesus

1. The Very Story is a going down (to humility, obedience, service, self-denial, or death) and a going up (to nearness to God, faith, redemption, or the life of God). What moments in your life may you regard as little copies of the Very Story?

2. What have been your hardest feelings in times of trouble and heartache? What elements of the gospel of Christ create the possibility of hope in such times?

3. When we hope, we rely on something outside our control to produce some good thing. It is easy to see that any particular hope might be futile, or it might be valid. For instance, to rely on a terminal illness to simply go away is a forlorn hope; it cannot be relied upon to do that. But to rely on God to bring some good thing out of even a terminal illness is a valid hope; he *can* be relied upon to do that. What hopes do you have, or have you had, involving God? What supports your faith that God can be relied upon for those things?

CHAPTER 9

Finding Your Way: Thoughts for the Journey

1. Read Ecclesiastes 3:1-8, which the *New International Version* titles "A Time for Everything." Think about each thing mentioned in this passage, and identify the ones that you yourself have experienced in the past year. Have you experienced both items in any pair? For instance, have you been touched by both a birth and a death? Have you both wept and laughed? How does the presence or absence of such "mixed pairs" affect your participation in the full range of human experience?

2. For the rest of this day, make a conscious effort to regard the sweet and the sour in your life as natural elements in human existence. If the sour results from things you can change, take steps to change them. Otherwise, accept them as part of being human.

3. Loss is one of the realities of life. Think of something you have lost that was once precious to you. While it is true that some things can never be replaced, think in terms of the principle, When God closes a door, he opens a window. What new thing has come into your life after the loss of the old?

ACTION STEPS

Moving Forward with the Trustworthy God

1. Pause at this moment and find one specific thing in your immediate surroundings to celebrate as a sign of God's goodness.

2. For this one day, resolve with vigor and boldness to base your life on what you know of the power and mercy of God, not on what you do not know and cannot know about the presence of evil.

3. Begin a journal as suggested in the section "Find Your Words" from chapter 9. Between yourself and God, develop honesty and truthfulness about your life, emotions, and faith.

4. Make a to-do list for today. Identify what makes you feel ready or not ready to do the things on this list. Decide whether these feelings are appropriate, whether they help you live bravely or timidly, whether they are based on faith or fear. Take steps to pace your readiness and unreadiness in a way that best enables your walk with God.

5. Ponder some issue that is facing you at present, something that you know will be a test or a challenge, something you do not gladly embark upon. Decide whether it can become an opportunity for growth and a means of drawing closer to the holy. This will help you decide whether to embark.

6. Look at the things you do for other people as well as the things you do for yourself. Evaluate your motivation in each case. Make an honest appraisal: Is this truly selfless? Is this truly selfish? Make changes accordingly.

7. During the next week provide yourself with opportunities both to be alone with God and to be with other people. If you feel

discomfort at either, think of how you might take steps to overcome your reluctance.

8. Place yourself in the hands of the trustworthy God through obedience to the gospel, and wake each morning with the thought, "Another day to follow the path of the One who always goes before!"

Notes

Dedication

The Greek phrase *tê epiterpôn hôrôn mnêmê* means "to the memory of happy times."

Preface: My End in My Beginning

1. Psalm 78:39.
2. See Ezekiel 37:1-10. This symbolism is easy and natural in the Bible, for the Hebrew word *ruach* means "wind," "breath," and "spirit."
3. Psalm 103:16.
4. John 3:8.

Chapter 1: The Meeting of Past and Future

1. See the larger Jacob narrative in Genesis 25:19–35:29. The story of Jacob wrestling through the night is found in Genesis 32:24-29.
2. Genesis 28:20-22.
3. Genesis 32:9-10.
4. Henry David Thoreau, *The Journal of Henry D. Thoreau*, ed. Bradford Torrey and Francis H. Allan, vol. 2 (New York: Dover, 1962), 1:457.
5. Jorge Luis Borges, "The Garden of Forking Paths," in *Labyrinths: Selected Stories and Other Writings*, ed. Donald A. Yates and James Irby (New York: New Directions, 1964), 28.

Chapter 2: At the Point of Turning

1. Psalm 142:6.

2. Psalm 40:11-12.

3. Psalm 41:3.

4. Psalm 139:14.

5. Psalm 38:6-8.

6. Job 3:20-21.

7. Job 7:4.

8. Job 7:16.

9. Job 1:21.

10. 2 Corinthians 1:3-5.

11. 1 Peter 5:10.

Chapter 3: In the Shadow of Mortality

1. Psalm 139:14.

2. See Psalms 6:5; 115:17.

3. We know little more about all this than is given in 1 Corinthians 15:35-58.

4. Two statements in the Psalms seem to run counter to this view. Psalm 49:15 says, "God will ransom my soul from the power of Sheol" (RSV), and Psalm 73:24 says (as familiarly known in the *King James Version*), "Afterward [thou shalt] receive me to glory." In the first instance, the meaning is probably that God will rescue the psalmist from premature death. In the second instance, the meaning is more like, "You will receive me with honor," perhaps as a ruler receives his servant. Whether this implies a life in heaven with God remains to be decided, and we are left with two fundamental possibilities: either the psalmist is using an image with no intentional reference to an afterlife, or else he is saying that his relationship with God will somehow transcend physical death. Either way, we are unjustified in finding highly developed conceptions of the afterlife among the ancient Israelites, because there is little tangible evidence that they had any and much evidence that they did not.

5. See Psalm 39:13.

6. Psalm 34:12.

7. Psalm 91:16.

8. Psalm 55:23.

9. Psalm 89:47.

10. Psalm 103:15-16.

11. I have taken these examples from whatever books were in the house. They not only illustrate the short-term approach to life, but they also show how widely distributed it is. They are, in order, Stephen Crane, poem 10 in *The Black Riders and Other Lines* (Boston: Copeland & Day, 1895); E. B. White, *Charlotte's Web* (New York: Harper & Row, 1952), 164; Horace, *Odes* 1.11 (23 B.C.); *The Epic of Gilgamesh* (2000 B.C.), Old Babylonian version, tablet 10, 3, in *Ancient Near Eastern Texts Relating to the Old Testament*, ed. James. B. Pritchard, trans. E. A. Speiser, 3d ed. (Princeton: Princeton University Press, 1969), 90; reprinted by permission of Princeton University Press. The wider context of the *Gilgamesh* quotation, by the way, exhibits similarities with Psalm 115:17; Ecclesiastes 5:18; 8:15; 9:8-9. The tablet on which it is written dates from the Old Babylonian period, 1750–1600 B.C., and is thus older than the biblical texts are likely to be. I think this shows how common the ideas were, rather than direct literary dependence.

12. *Epic of Gilgamesh*, Assyrian version, tablet 10, 6, in *Ancient Near Eastern Texts*, 92.

13. See especially Ecclesiastes 2:24; 8:15; 9:8-9.

Chapter 4: The Choice for Praise

1. Psalm 37:4, KJV.

2. Psalm 19:14, KJV.

3. Psalm 25:4, KJV.

4. Psalms 88:6; 102:5; 58:8, RSV.

5. See Psalm 6:5.

6. See Psalms 7:8; 17:3.

7. See Psalm 35:13-16.

8. Possidius, *The Life of Saint Augustine,* 31, trans. F. R. Hoare in *The Western Fathers* (New York: Sheed & Ward, 1954; reprint, New York: Harper & Row, 1965), 242.

9. Psalm 32:5.

10. Psalm 38:18.

11. Psalm 51:3.

12. Psalm 6:6-7.

13. Psalm 38:7-8.

14. Psalm 102:3-7.

15. The Hebrew word *Yahweh* is the personal name by which ancient Israel addressed God. In later times the name Yahweh came not to be spoken, and a term meaning "Lord" was substituted. In English Bibles, with few exceptions, the word *Lord* is consistently used to represent the name Yahweh.

16. Psalms 77:13; 96:5.

17. Psalm 47:2,7-8.

18. See Psalm 95:5.

19. See Psalms 97:1-5; 29:3-9.

20. See Psalms 96:13; 98:9.

21. See Psalm 103:19-22.

22. Isaiah 57:15. In Exodus 3:13-15, the name Yahweh is related to the divine disclosure, I AM WHO I AM. In Hebrew, there is a verbal similarity between the two expressions that cannot be shown easily in English. For my description of biblical monotheism in this paragraph, I am indebted to Patrick D. Miller, *The Religion of Ancient Israel,* Library of Ancient Israel, ed. Douglas A. Knight (London: SPCK; Louisville, Ky.: John Knox, 2000), esp. 7-14; and Walter Brueggemann, *Old Testament*

Theology: Essays on Structures, Theme, and Text, ed. Patrick D. Miller (Minneapolis: Fortress, 1992), 118-49.

23. Psalm 46:1. See also 18:2; 19:14.

24. Psalm 31:2.

25. Psalms 32:11; 20:5.

26. Psalm 40:3,9, RSV.

27. Psalms 6:3; 13:1; 74:10.

28. Psalm 42:9.

29. Psalm 43:2.

30. Psalm 77:7-10. See also 10:1; 44:23-24; 69:17.

31. For examples, see Psalms 35; 41; 55:12-15.

32. See Psalms 38:3-4; 39:11.

33. The psalmists feel the pain of this, of course, but accept it as appropriate. What does bother them, however, is that often the choice for wickedness seems to lead to prosperity and comfort. See Psalms 37:7; 73:3,12-14; 82:2.

34. Isaiah 45:7. I have cited this verse in the plain and blunt wording of the *King James Version.* The statement that God creates "evil" does not mean that God is culpable of moral wickedness. That is totally against the point that Isaiah is making. But it does mean that God's power and will are absolute, that nothing is out of his control, and therefore, that he is ultimately responsible for whatever happens, whether prosperity or "disaster" (NIV), weal or "woe" (RSV). This is what cannot be softened.

35. Psalm 88:7.

36. Psalm 88:16.

37. Psalm 39:10,7.

38. Psalm 38:1-2,22. See also Psalms 60:1-3; 80:4-5.

39. Artur Weiser, *The Psalms,* trans. Herbert Hartwell, Old Testament Library (London: SCM, 1962), 325.

40. Psalm 16:2.

41. Psalm 73:25,28.

42. Psalm 119:175.

43. Psalm 63:4.

44. "A Simple Song," from *Mass: A Theatre Piece for Singers, Players and Dancers,* music by Leonard Bernstein; text from the liturgy of the Roman Mass; additional texts by Stephen Schwartz and Leonard Bernstein (New York: Jalni Publications/Boosey & Hawkes, 1971).

Chapter 5: Against the Wind

1. Job 1:1.

2. Job 1:6. NIV translates this as "angels," but I prefer the more literal wording, "sons of God," as in RSV and elsewhere.

3. Job 1:9-11. The words that the Accuser has just spoken contain a word-play in the Hebrew text. The word translated *curse* normally means "bless." If we were to translate the Accuser's words literally, we might do so as follows: "Job will surely 'bless' you to your face." In this sentence, *bless* is a euphemism. The storyteller wishes to avoid saying that Job will curse God, for heaven forbid that anyone should curse God! (And you see that now in saying "heaven forbid," we have used yet another euphemism.) So the author writes *bless,* although *curse* is what he means. It happens several times throughout this story that the word *bless* sometimes means "bless" and sometimes "curse." When Job says, "Blessed be the name of the LORD" (1:21, RSV), it is ironic that he is saying just what the Accuser said he would, only he really does mean "bless." When Job's wife tells him to "curse" God and die, she is using this same word too. Irony follows irony. Not only can blessings and cursings come from the same mouth, they can come from the same *word.*

4. Job 1:22.

5. Job 1:21, RSV.

6. Job 2:4.

7. Job 2:5.

8. Job 2:6.

9. Job 30:16.

10. Job 2:7.

11. Job 2:9.

12. Job 2:10.

13. As in Job 12.

Chapter 6: The Unraveling of Reason

1. Alvin Moscow, *Collision Course* (New York: Putnam, 1959), 85.

2. Job 4:8.

3. Job 5:11-12,17-18.

4. Job 42:7.

5. Job 16:3; 13:4; 16:2.

6. Job 38:4,12,16-17,34,39; 39:26.

7. See Job 40:7-14.

8. See Job 40:4.

9. Job 42:5.

10. See Job 42:6.

Chapter 7: The God of Thick Darkness

1. Juxtaposing two petitions in Psalm 38:2,22.

2. *Lord* is the highest name, for it is the name of God. The hymnlike passage is found in Philippians 2:5-11.

3. In the preaching of the early church, the Resurrection showed Jesus to be God's Son descended from David (see Romans 1:3-4); it fulfilled God's promises to the patriarchs of Israel (see Acts 13:32-33); and it glorified his servant Jesus (see Acts 3:13-15). These are major themes in the faith of Israel—sonship, promise, servanthood—and the resurrection of Jesus meant that Israel's faith had been affirmed.

4. Acts 3:13.

5. Mark 14:34, echoing language from Psalms 42:5-6,11; 43:5. Psalms 42 and 43 are wrongly divided. Together they constitute a single psalm.

6. George Hedley, *The Symbol of the Faith: A Study of the Apostles' Creed* (New York: Macmillan, 1948), 60-2.

7. Mark 14:33.

8. Mark 14:35-36.

9. Mark 14:41.

10. Matthew 26:39,42.

11. Mark 15:34 and Matthew 27:46, both of which cite words from Psalm 22:1.

12. Excerpted from Psalm 22:1-2,4,6,9,11,15-16,18-19,22-24,27.

13. Mark 8:34; Matthew 16:24; and Luke 9:23. The wording in the gospel of Luke makes it even more clear that this is a call, not to a remote possibility, but to a way of life, for the follower of Jesus must take up his cross "daily."

Chapter 8: The Future of Hope

1. 1 Peter 5:10.

2. Job 42:10-17. The book of Job is saved from the charge of contrivance if we see the plot as a very wealthy man passing through the mixed contents of his life. We, too, experience the same fluctuation from high to low to high again, although usually not to Job's extreme degree—but then we are not Oriental potentates!

3. Hebrews 11:33-35, RSV.

4. See Luke 24:25-27; John 20:21-23; Matthew 28:16-20 parallels Mark 16:14-18; Luke 24:44-49; John 21:15-19; Acts 1:1-8; 9:3-6 parallels 22:6-10, which parallels 26:13-18.

5. Matthew Arnold, "Dover Beach," in *New Poems* (London: MacMillan, 1867). This short but complex poem concerns loss of faith in a confused

and bewildering time and two lovers' retreat to the solution of the short run. The speaker calls his beloved to the window above the shore:

Listen! you hear the grating roar
Of pebbles which the waves draw back, and fling,
At their return, up the high strand.

The sound of the water withdrawing over the pebbles on the beach had been heard by the Greek dramatist Sophocles, "and it brought / Into his mind the turbid ebb and flow / Of human misery." For Arnold the sound brings another thought to mind. The "Sea of Faith / Was once, too, at the full."

But now I only hear
Its melancholy, long, withdrawing roar,
Retreating, to the breath
Of the night wind, down the vast edges drear
And naked shingles of the world.

Since there is only futility in the world and faith itself is ebbing away, the speaker appeals to his beloved that they cling all the more to each other:

Ah, love, let us be true
To one another! for the world...
Hath neither joy, nor love, nor light,
Nor certitude, nor peace, nor help for pain.

I cite this poem at some length, for it is a lucid and powerful depiction of life's movement of descent—but without the Very Story's message of hope and redemption.

6. John 12:24.
7. See John 12:25-26.

8. See Luke 6:38; Acts 20:35.

9. See Mark 9:35; 10:15.

10. See Mark 8:34-38.

11. See Matthew 5:3-12.

12. See Romans 6:3-4.

13. See Ephesians 5:21–6:9.

14. See James 2:5.

15. See Philippians 2:5.

16. George MacDonald, "The Consuming Fire," in *Unspoken Sermons Series One* (London: Alexander Strahan, 1867).

17. Martin Luther King Jr., "Suffering and Faith," *Christian Century* 77 (27 April 1960): 510. Reprinted in *A Testament of Hope: The Essential Writings of Martin Luther King, Jr.,* ed. James Melvin Washington (San Francisco: HarperSanFrancisco, 1986), 41-2.

18. When the word *hope* has a religious meaning, it means to hope *in God.* That is, hope is confident reliance upon God to bring about some good thing in keeping with his character and promise. Thus, when God promised offspring to Abraham and Sarah in their old age, "against all hope, Abraham in hope believed" (Romans 4:18). Thus we "take hold of the hope offered to us," and our hope is "an anchor for the soul, firm and secure" (Hebrews 6:18-19). Christian hope is not limited to this world only (1 Corinthians 15:19); because of the resurrection of Jesus, the church's "faith and hope" are in the God who raised him (1 Peter 1:21) and will ultimately be brought to fulfillment when "Jesus Christ is revealed" (1 Peter 1:13; also see Colossians 1:5).

19. See 1 Corinthians 15:35-58.

Chapter 9: Finding Your Way

1. Gerard Manley Hopkins, "Pied Beauty," in *Poems of Gerard Manley Hopkins,* ed. Robert Bridges (London: Humphrey Milford, 1918).

2. See especially Ecclesiastes 3:1-8.

3. Ecclesiastes 3:9.

4. Ecclesiastes 12:13-14.

5. Philippians 4:11-13.

6. Psalm 102:25-26.

7. Walt Whitman, "There Was a Child Went Forth," in *Leaves of Grass,* 1891–92 ed. (Philadelphia: David McKay, 1891), 282.

8. From an interview in *Writers at Work: The* Paris Review *Interviews,* 8th series, ed. George Plimpton (New York: Viking Penguin, 1988), 22.

9. Robert Louis Stevenson, *Kidnapped* (London: Cassell; New York: Scribners, 1886), chap. 20.

10. Matthew 6:6, NEB.

11. Rabi'a of Basra, quoted in J. H. Bavinck, *The Impact of Christianity on the Non-Christian World* (Grand Rapids: Eerdmans, 1948), 46.

12. C. S. Lewis, *The Four Loves* (New York: Harcourt Brace Jovanovich, 1960), 80.

13. *Nicomachean Ethics* 9.4. "Another you" is how we would express it informally today. Aristotle's *allos autos,* "another self," has been turned into Latin as *alter ego,* and you will sometimes encounter this expression in English writing, meaning "a trusted friend." Aristotle's discussion of friendship may be read in J. A. K. Thomson, *The Ethics of Aristotle: The Nicomachean Ethics Translated* (London: George Allen & Unwin, 1953), 239-41.

14. You will find it in Aristophanes' speech, *Symposium* 189C-192E, trans. W. R. M. Lamb, Loeb Classical Library (Cambridge: Harvard University Press, 1925), 133-45. If you look it up, you will find that Aristophanes has loaded the story with erotic possibilities along ancient Hellenic lines. But as even he recognized, eroticism is not essential to the story: "No one," he says, "could imagine…that such alone could be the reason why each rejoices in the other's company" (p. 143).

15. See Romans 6:1-14.

16. See John 17:13-19.

17. See 1 Thessalonians 4:13-14.

18. 2 Corinthians 1:3-5.

Resources

SCRIPTURE

Isaiah 40. A message of comfort for Israel. Voices from heaven declare comfort and pardon (40:1-11) from the Lord who is Creator and Master of the universe (40:12-26) and who cares for his people (40:27-31).

Jeremiah 11:18–12:6; 15:10-21; 17:14-18; 18:18-23; 20:7-13,14-18. These passages are called collectively the "confessions" of Jeremiah. With more justification, they might be called Jeremiah's "laments," for they are similar to the personal laments found in the Psalms. In his laments, Jeremiah vents his rage, frustration, and fear, and at times he comes close to blasphemy. And yet, in his grief and pain he hears the voice of God.

Jeremiah 30–31. A message of hope and restoration after Israel's darkest days.

Lamentations. Communal laments written by an eyewitness to the fall of Jerusalem in 587 B.C. This book expresses the people's agony in response to the tragedy as well as the hope that God will work his purposes for the future.

Habakkuk. Alone among the prophets, Habakkuk addresses his oracle to God, not to us. He confronts God with the question: "Why dost thou look on faithless men, and art silent when the wicked swallows up the man more righteous than he?" (1:13, RSV). God's answer is that he is in fact working out his justice, but all in good time, and in the meanwhile, "the righteous shall live by his faith" (2:4, RSV).

The book ends with the prophet's declaration of trust, one of the loveliest in Scripture (3:17-19).

Matthew 5:3-12. The Beatitudes. Blessedness is the true happiness that God gives. Those whose future is full of hope are those who live the life of God even on the downhill slope.

Acts 2:14-42; 10:34-48. The gospel proclaimed by the early church. The clearest call of promise and hope for all humankind.

2 Corinthians 1:3-7. Paul's usual epistolary thanksgiving is here addressed to our God "of all comfort." As we share in Christ's sufferings, we share in comfort, too.

Revelation 7:13-17; 22:1-5. In vivid picture writing, these passages show John's vision of those who have passed through earthly troubles and have come into the presence of God.

BOOKS

Allender, Dan, and Tremper Longman III. *The Cry of the Soul: How Our Emotions Reveal Our Deepest Questions About God.* Colorado Springs: NavPress, 1999. A counselor and a theologian collaborate on a book about the Psalms. The authors show that profound human emotion can lead to profound religious experience.

Blocher, Henri. *Evil and the Cross.* Translated by David G. Preston. Downers Grove, Ill.: InterVarsity, 1994. After surveying and evaluating proposed intellectual solutions to the problem of evil, Blocher concludes that none is adequate. Evil is not explained; it is defeated in the cross of Christ.

Bonar, Horatius. *When God's Children Suffer.* Grand Rapids: Kregel, 1992.

Clarkson, Margaret. *Destined for Glory: The Meaning of Suffering.* Grand Rapids: Eerdmans, 1983.

Gowan, Donald E. *The Triumph of Faith in Habakkuk*. Atlanta: John Knox, 1976. Informed by the scholarly study of this small Old Testament book, but presented for the general reader who has asked, "Why, in a world governed by a good God, does wickedness so often triumph?"

Johnson, Spencer. *The Precious Present*. New York: Doubleday, 1984. A little boy discovers what the present is and why it is precious.

Lewis, C. S. *A Grief Observed*. San Francisco: HarperSanFrancisco, 2001. During his short marriage to Joy Davidman, Lewis remarked to a friend, "I never expected to have, in my sixties, the happiness that passed me by in my twenties." In the months following Joy's death, Lewis recorded the feelings of grief, fear, and rage that make up this small book. The book's honesty in expressing these feelings is the reason it has been a consolation to so many readers.

———. *The Problem of Pain*. San Francisco: HarperSanFrancisco, 2001. A discussion of why misery exists in a world created by a good and all-powerful God. Lewis writes as a scholar and logician, but the book is short and not difficult to read.

Lloyd-Jones, D. Martyn. *Why Does God Allow Suffering?* Wheaton, Ill.: Crossway, 1994. First published in 1939 at the outbreak of war in Europe. Lloyd-Jones locates the "most comprehensive, and the most final, answer" in Romans 8:28.

McGuiggan, Jim. *Celebrating the Wrath of God: Reflections on the Agony and the Ecstasy of His Relentless Love*. Colorado Springs: WaterBrook, 2001.

Marty, Martin E. *A Cry of Absence: Reflections for the Winter of the Heart*. Grand Rapids: Eerdmans, 1997. A meditation on the text of the

Psalms. The book addresses people who struggle with pain, trouble, and loss, but whose "wintry" style of spirituality and faith is not responsive to the more exuberant and triumphant style of "summery" faith.

Stackhouse Jr., John G. *Can God Be Trusted? Faith and the Challenge of Evil.* New York: Oxford University Press, 2000. A thoughtful and intelligent approach. Stackhouse concedes that we will find no comprehensive answer to the question of evil. But we can nonetheless decide with good reason whether God can be trusted.

Swinburne, Richard. *Providence and the Problem of Evil.* Oxford: Oxford University Press, 1998. Conversational and philosophical at the same time, this book maintains that suffering cannot be avoided in a world where the good of the individual is "to choose between good and evil...to develop their own characters...to show courage and loyalty, to love, to be of use, to contemplate beauty and discover truth," and voluntarily to serve and adore God.

Lord Tennyson, Alfred. *In Memoriam.* Edited by Susan Shatto and Marion Shaw. Oxford: Oxford University Press, 1982. Lyric poems expressing Tennyson's wide range of feelings from grief to despair to hope, prompted by the death of his closest friend, Arthur Hallam.

Wenham, John W. *The Enigma of Evil: Can We Believe in the Goodness of God?* Grand Rapids: Zondervan, 1985. Belief in the goodness of God is challenged by severities in both Scripture and experience. But Christ shows that God is not merely severe, he is kind.

Yancey, Philip. *Where Is God When It Hurts?* Grand Rapids: Zondervan, 2002. Pain is the body's warning system, but what do we make of misery and suffering? A biblical perspective.

MUSIC

Dorothea von Ertmann was a fine pianist and a friend of Beethoven. When she suffered the loss of one of her children, Beethoven—socially awkward at best—did not at first want to see her. Finally, he invited her to visit him. When she came he sat down at the piano and said, "Now we will talk to one another in tones." For more than an hour he played without stopping, and she remarked, "He told me everything and at last brought me comfort."

When we are in sorrow, music has the ability to comfort and console our hearts, to express and to evoke deep emotions, and to open our spirits to renewed hope in the possibility of beauty and goodness. In the following short list are musical works that have brought meaning and comfort to people in their grief:

"Be Thou My Vision." Traditional Irish words and melody.

van Beethoven, Ludwig. Symphony No. 2. Beethoven wrote this joyous and capricious symphony at the same time he was dealing emotionally with his increasing deafness. He contemplated suicide but chose life for the sake of making music like this.

———. Symphony No. 9. The last movement contains the famous "Ode to Joy."

Byrd, William. Motets and anthems.

Cowper, William. "God Moves in a Mysterious Way." Although gripped by periods of despondency and emotional turmoil, Cowper wrote some of the best-known hymns in the English language. This one captures the balance between the mystery and kindness of God.

Fauré, Gabriel. *Requiem.* As a church organist for much of his career, Fauré developed definite ideas about what sort of music best speaks to people in times of grief and loss. His requiem, composed within

the same two-year period in which he suffered the loss of both his
parents, is tender, compassionate, and hopeful.

Górecki, Henryk. Symphony No. 3. Although this work bears the
subtitle "Symphony of Sorrowful Songs," its overall impression
is not sorrowful. It is radiant with hope.

Handel, George Frideric. *Messiah.* More than a Christmas musical, this
oratorio sweeps from the prophecies of Isaiah to the coming of
Christ to the Last Judgment and the angels' song of praise.

Lyte, Henry F. "Abide with Me."

Mahler, Gustav. Symphony No. 2, "Resurrection."

———. Symphony No. 5. During one early vigil in the hospital, I had
a little tape player and a recording of this music that a friend had
given me. As I listened to the slow fourth movement, I was overwhelmed by the realization that someone, somewhere, sometime,
had taken his profound sorrow and despair and turned it into music
of such beauty and power.

Mozart, Wolfgang Amadeus. *Requiem.*

Newman, John Henry. "Lead, Kindly Light." Newman wrote this hymn
on a return voyage from Italy, when he was disturbed with doubts
but confident of God's power to lead.

Newton, John. "Amazing Grace." Among the original stanzas of this
hymn is one not ordinarily found in modern hymnals:

The earth shall soon dissolve like snow,
　　The sun forbear to shine;
But God, who call'd me here below,
　　Will be forever mine.

Smetana, Bedřich. *The Moldau.* A tone-poem depicting the course of the
River Moldau from its sources to its majestic full breadth. A friend
of mine says that at her funeral there will be not one spoken word;

people will simply listen to *The Moldau* and depart in silence and in peace.

Tavener, John. *Lamentations and Praises.* A setting of texts for the Orthodox service of Good Friday, commissioned by the vocal ensemble Chanticleer. The composer conceived the work as something to be both seen and heard, full of "gladdening sorrow."